Thank you for
participation —
Love, Susan
December 2014

1

Editors - Family

Mark Ainley and Vicky Ainley, Vancouver, 2014

Editors - Colleagues

On June 28, 2014, we met in Baie D'Urfe, QC, to help bring together the following volume. Some of us are in regular contact, others not as much, given time, distance and personal lives. We bonded again quickly, and spent eight hours planning and editing. The topic of birding inevitably came up: we thought about *A Bird in the Bush*, by Margaret Pye Arnaudin. She was a long-time birder and friend of Marika's. In her own words, "There was always another path of exploration to go down, always one more person to interview." Let us continue the work.

Left to right: Susan Hoecker-Drysdale, E. Tina Crossfield, Mary E. Baldwin, Anne-Marie Weidler Kubanek

Marika dressed for a Victorian wedding, April 2006, Victoria, B.C.

Remembering MARIKA

Marianne Gosztonyi Ainley
1937-2008

Editors: E. Tina Crossfield, Susan Hoecker-Drysdale, Anne-Marie Weidler Kubanek, Mary Baldwin, Vicky Ainley, and Mark Ainley

October 2014

ISBN-13: 978-0968664643

ISBN-10: 0968664644

Editors: E. Tina Crossfield, Susan Hoecker-Drysdale, Anne-Marie Weidler Kubanek, Mary E. Baldwin, Vicky Ainley and Mark Ainley

Cover design, layout and illustration by Harald Kunze

Crossfield Publishing   www.crossfieldpublishing.ca

2269 Road 120, R7, St. Marys, Ontario, N4X 1C9, Canada

1-226-301-4001

Cataloguing in Publication

1. Biography, 2. Memoir, 3. Science, 4. History, 5. Ornithology, 6. Women's Studies, 7. Feminism, 8. University

Cover photo Courtesy of The (Montreal) Gazette, Dave Sidaway, April 15, 1988

"It's Spring and we are on the trail of the Dark-eyed Junco and other beauties" Published May 1, 1988, article by Mark Abley

Cover artwork by Marianne G. Ainley: front - Southern Galaxy; back - Sunset Over Lake Taupo

A portion of the proceeds from the sale of this book are to be donated to *Bird Protection Quebec* in memory of Marianne Gosztonyi Ainley.

CROSSFIELD
PUBLISHING

Dedication

Marianne sought to encourage and inspire those around her to expand their horizons and do their work, regardless of the opposition or attempts to silence them. She spent decades discovering and celebrating people whose work had gone unrecognized or unappreciated. Additionally, she was able to recognize people's innate talents and how they might use them professionally.

This book is therefore dedicated to those who have their sights set on vistas not yet travelled, who have felt obstructed in their work, and whose talents have not yet found a focused avenue of expression. May you find the strength and courage within to navigate your path with fortitude and enthusiasm.

Muriwai View

Table of Contents

Mount Tolmie Sunset

Foreword

MARIANNE (MARIKA) GOSZTONYI AINLEY
1937 – 2008
by Mary E. Baldwin

Marianne Gosztonyi Ainley's path from laboratory technician to eminent historian of Canadian science, bridging a gap in Canadian women's history, is a remarkable one. She was in her late forties when she began her research career, and held a salaried position relevant to her field for only eleven years, yet made significant contributions.

Marika Gosztonyi was born in Budapest on December 4th, 1937. She grew up in Hungary during the Second World War and under the Communist regime, completing a four-year Diploma of Industrial Chemistry in 1956 at the Petrik Lajos Polytechnical College of Chemistry, Budapest. She left Hungary following the 1956 uprising, and came as an immigrant to Canada, settling in Montreal. In the early years in Montreal she worked in various laboratories as a technician and later as a research assistant while completing her Bachelor of Arts degree at night school at what was then Sir George Williams University (now Concordia University), with concentrations in English and French literature. In 1966 she married David Ainley, a high school teacher from Yorkshire who taught within the Protestant School Board of Montreal.

We met in the fall of 1966 in the Chemistry Department of Loyola College, Montreal, which since 1974 has been part of Concordia University. She had just begun working as a research assistant for Dr. Tom Nogrady, a fellow Hungarian, and I was working as a laboratory instructor. Loyola College at that time was a four-year college run by the Jesuits, and there were very few women who were not office staff. We shared the difficulties of being isolated professional women in science and working mothers with young children; we were both immigrants who had experienced discrimination against married women in the workplace, and the problems of qualifications from another country.

During the late sixties Marianne became increasingly frustrated with the role of research assistant, where one's contribution to a project may be substantial but receive little recognition, and there was little freedom to pursue one's own research ideas. She was very interested in anthropology, and had been accepted into a Masters program when life intervened in 1969 with the birth of her son, Mark. Graduate school was put on hold, and she was at home for several years while her son was a young child, finding creative outlets through pottery and birding as an observational field study. She was active in the local birding community becoming a Director of the Province of Quebec Society for the Protection of Birds from 1973 until 1995 when she left Montreal. She joined the American Ornithological Union in 1972, and was a member of their Centennial Committee in 1982-83. She completed Cornell University's Certificate in Ornithology in 1979, and birding remained a lifelong passion.

Marianne returned to work in the Loyola Chemistry Department in 1974, first as a research assistant and later as a laboratory instructor for General Chemistry, but did not give up on the notion of graduate school. A chemistry colleague, Dr. Michael Hogben, who was head of Interdisciplinary Studies at Loyola at the time, suggested to her to investigate the History of Science program at Université de Montréal. She had found her field, and enrolled in the Institut d'histoire et de sociopolitique des sciences at Université de Montréal in 1978. There, she was able to combine her interest in the scientific contributions of amateurs and her love of ornithology, and completed an M.Sc. under the supervision of Dr. Lewis Pyenson in 1980 with the thesis "La professionalisation de l'ornithologie Américaine 1870 –1979". This was a real triumph, as seminars and all theses at Université de Montréal were in French, a third language for her; this experience greatly enhanced her French/English bilingualism. She received a doctoral fellowship from FCAC Quebec, and moved to McGill University, Montreal, to complete her PhD in the History and Philosophy of Science under the direction of Dr. Maxwell J. Dunbar. She expanded on the work she had begun in ornithology, on the professionalization of this field science, the role and contributions of amateurs, and issues of colonialism and science, receiving her degree in 1985 for her dissertation: "From Natural History to Avian Biology: Canadian Ornithology 1860-1950".

The work for her graduate degrees required extensive archival research across Canada, and interviews with those still alive who were involved in ornithology prior to 1950, and with their descendants for insights and information. These field trips for research were combined with the family camping trips during the summer school holidays. This pattern of travel and research has continued across the years – summer camping trips during school holidays with travel destinations built around visits to archives and libraries in Canada and the US, and interviews with people relevant to the current research project.

In 1985, following completion of her doctorate, Marianne received a grant from the Canadian Social Sciences and Humanities Research Council (SSHRC) as an Independent Researcher to work on a scientific biography of William Rowan, a British trained ornithologist, who came to Canada to establish the Zoology Department at the University of Alberta. In the course of her doctoral research she had become very interested in his experimental work on bird migration, the problems he encountered as a field researcher, and his role as a popular communicator of science through radio, and felt strongly that his contributions and experiences should be more widely known. However, research grants in Canada do not provide income to the individual, and there were few academic positions available in the 1980s. It was also very difficult at that time, before e-mail and the internet, to be an independent researcher without an institutional affiliation to provide a base, access to libraries and archives, colleagues for discussion and collaboration etc. She did complete the biography "Restless Energy – A Biography of William Rowan, 1891—1957" (Véhicule Press, Montreal, 1993) which was published with a SSHRC publication grant.

Meanwhile Marianne's research in Canadian history of science changed focus. SSHRC's Women and Work program had just been introduced, and she recognized this was a potential source to fund research on the work of Canadian women in science. Margaret Rossiter's book "Women Scientists in America: Struggles and Strategies to 1940" was published in 1982 but at that time there was little published historical information about Canadian women scientists, although Marianne had come across women naturalists in her graduate work. She received a small research grant for 1984-85 from the Canadian Institute for the Advancement of Women to work on: "Canadian Women Natural Scientists: A Pilot Project", and a SSHRC post- doctoral fellowship in '85-'86 to work on History of Canadian Women in Science, which she spent in the History Department at McGill University. In 1986 she obtained the first of two SSHRC major strategic grants covering 1986-92 for Women and Scientific Work, which set the direction for her future research, again as an Independent Scholar, which was highly unusual.

Marianne still sought an institutional affiliation, and in late 1986 I introduced her to Arpi Hamalian, the Principal of the Simone de Beauvoir Institute, Concordia University, who suggested that she become a Research Fellow of the Institute. This was the start of her association with the Simone de Beauvoir Institute, and involvement with the Women's Studies program at Concordia, which was housed within the Institute. In 1988 she began teaching part-time in the program, developing a course in Historical and Contemporary Perspectives of Women, Science and Technology. In June during a discussion we had of her difficulties locating Canadian reading material for her course, the idea was conceived that she should create a book to fill this gap. So she solicited and edited a series of essays to which she also contributed, and, in 1990, "Despite the Odds: Essays on Canadian Women and Science" (Véhicule Press, Montreal) was published. This anthology reflected a broad view of science, and illustrated the wide range of scientific activities engaged in by Canadian women in the nineteenth and early twentieth centuries, highlighting their accomplishments while underlining the many difficulties encountered.

In 1989 she was an Associate Scholar, History of Science Society (U.S.) and she spent 1990 at Carlton University, Ottawa, as a Visiting Scholar in their Women's Studies program. In 1991 she became Principal of the Simone de Beauvoir Institute, and Director and Associate Professor, Women's Studies at Concordia University where she remained for the next four years. This was her first salaried full time position. During this period she provided dynamic leadership to the Institute, introducing innovations in the curriculum and teaching methods, organizing research seminars and fostering collaborations with colleagues in other departments and universities. She herself was actively involved in collaborations on oral history, feminist research methods, and feminist biography. She was also a co-investigator in a SSHRC strategic grant "Women Engineers Within and Outside the Profession."

In 1995 the opportunity to become Professor and Chair of Women's Studies at the new University of Northern British Columbia (UNBC) in Prince George, B.C., provided a fresh challenge and a secure tenured academic position. This was a major move, supported by David, who was able to take retirement from the Protestant School Board of Greater Montreal, where he had taught for more than 30 years. At UNBC Marianne had the opportunity to shape their Women's Studies Program, develop a graduate M.A. program in Gender Studies, and supervise graduate students working in Gender Studies, Environmental Studies and First

Nation Studies. She developed courses on "Feminist Perspectives on Science and Technology", " Women and the Environment: Historical and Contemporary Perspectives", "Gender, Power and Environmental Problems", and "Changing Methods: Scholarship, Gender and Transforming practices". She loved teaching and working with her graduate students, encouraging and advising them on their research projects. Her teaching received external recognition with the Teaching as if the World Mattered Award in 2001 in Toronto from the Biology as if the World Mattered Research Group. Her outstanding contribution to UNBC has been recognized, as she was made Professor Emerita at a special ceremony held there in 2005.

Following her mandatory retirement at sixty-five in 2002, Marianne and David moved to Victoria, British Columbia. There she actively continued her research and writing projects, and developed as an artist – she had started to paint as a creative outlet while in Prince George, and painted and exhibited regularly in Victoria with the Madrona group of women artists.

Marianne was a productive and well-funded scholar. History of women and scientific work in Canada has been one of the main themes of her research, which branched in many directions. At UNBC, her research expanded to the relationship between women and the environment, and issues related to the transfer and recognition of First Nations environmental knowledge during colonial times, exploring the cultural parallels between the Australian, New Zealand and Canadian experience. In 2000 she went to Australia as Distinguished Professorial Visitor at the Centre for Social Science Research at Central Queensland University in Rockhampton, and in 2001 she went to New Zealand as Visiting Scholar at the Institute for Study of Gender at Auckland University. In 2001 she received a SSHRC grant to work on "Re-explorations: new perspectives on gender, environment and transfer of knowledge in 19th and 20th century Canada and Australia". In conjunction with this research she spent time in Australia in 2003 as a Visiting Scholar at the Australian National University in Canberra, and also at Central Queensland University. She returned again to Australia in 2006 as a Visiting Scholar at the Alcoa Research Centre for Stronger Communities at Curtain University in Perth, Western Australia.

In addition to her own books, she has contributed more than 20 book chapters to other collections, as well as numerous articles in peer reviewed journals on issues in the history of women in science in Canada, as well as on Canadian ornithology. She made contributions to the Oxford Companion to Canadian History, the Biographical Dictionary of North American Environmentalists, and the New Oxford Dictionary of National Biography. She was sought after as a book reviewer, reviewing books on history of science, women in science, and ornithology for a broad range of journals.

Marianne gave back generously to her profession; she was elected for three terms as President of the Canadian Science and Technology Historical Association, from 1993 to 1999, and was also President of the Canadian Women's Studies Association in 1999 to 2000. She served as a member of the editorial board of Scientia Canadensis, and was a referee for SSHRC. Marianne believed strongly in sharing the ideas and the insights which she developed. She not only made regular conference presentations, and organized symposia at scholarly meetings in both History of Science and Women's Studies, but also was frequently invited as a speaker to a wide range of other disciplinary and interdisciplinary gatherings. For the past twenty years she was a mentor to many who were interested in increasing our knowledge and understanding of Canadian women's contribution in science.

She also worked to bridge the gap between the community and the academy, particularly during her time at Prince George, contributing her expertise to exhibitions accessible to the wider public. Her first experience was as the organizer of the "History of Canadian Ornithology" exhibition at the Redpath Museum, McGill University in 1991. She curated a number of historical exhibits of Canadian achievements in science both at Concordia and at UNBC. She served as the UNBC community member of the organizing committee for the UNBC Arts Council and Prince George Art Gallery exhibition "Other Eyes: Art, Racism and Stereotypes" in 1998, and for the Prince George Art Gallery exhibition "Body Image" in 1999. From 1993-95 she served on the Advisory Panel for the Ontario Science Centre project "Whose Science Is It?" in Toronto, and from 1996-98 was a member of the Selection Committee for the Canadian Science and Engineering Hall of Fame, at the National Museum of Science and Technology, Ottawa.

Most recently, since retirement and despite illness, she had finally completed and submitted for publication the book synthesizing many years of historical research on Canadian women scientists in academia. She received the first reviews of the manuscript "Overlooked Dimensions: Women and Scientific Work at Canadian Universities 1884-1980" suggesting some revisions late in the summer of 2008, but sadly was not able to complete them. It is my hope that her book will be published, so that this valuable work becomes available to other scholars. In the summer of 2005 Marianne was diagnosed with breast cancer, but continued with her research throughout the treatments, maintaining a positive outlook and accomplishing a great deal during periods of remission. She died peacefully in Victoria surrounded by her family on September 26, 2008.

Marianne had enormous energy, but her career would not have been possible without the love and support of her husband David and her children, Vicky and Mark. David provided encouragement through all the difficult times and frustrations. He drove countless miles across the years enabling her research on a shoestring while sharing her love of nature and photographing birds. He was, she always told me, the best editor of her work, ensuring clear use of language.

Marianne was a wonderful, vibrant, warm and colorful friend to many people. She gave generously to friends, colleagues and students, providing encouragement and support in their various scholarly and artistic pursuits, and her life had a ripple effect on the lives of those who knew her. For me, the titles of her books in many ways reflect her life – she herself was full of restless energy and her career is an example of what can be accomplished in scholarship and creativity despite the odds.

Postscript:

The above account of Marianne's life and work was written in 2009. My hope that her final manuscript would be published has now been fulfilled. At the request of Jean Wilson, formerly of University of British Columbia press, Geoff and Marelene Rayner-Canham kindly undertook the editing to bring the manuscript to publishable state, not changing the content and being careful as they state in their editorial note "not to amend Marianne's voice or narrative in any way". *Creating Complicated Lives: Women and Science at English-Canadian Universities, 1880-1980* was published in 2012 by McGill-Queen's University Press.

Uluru

Family

WITH LOVE AND PAPRIKA
Vicky Ainley

I remember my Mother using a cookbook entitled, Cooking with Love and Paprika! It was of course a Hungarian cookbook and I've always thought that it also described her in a way. Lots of love and lots of Paprika! Passion, perfection, compassion, adventure, affection, energy, drive and dedication! She even coloured her hair every shade of Paprika!

Although she has been described as hot and spicy, she was to me a really cool mother. By cool, I of course mean progressive. She essentially encouraged me to be the independent woman that I am and I really owe a lot of it to her. I know now that she made a difference in the lives of so many women through her work in Women's Studies at various universities, but she didn't neglect to do the same at home.

Mother-daughter relationships are very special. It is almost impossible to describe it in words, but I think that is what made our relationship beautiful, in that she understood and respected me. We were friends and she confided in me as well. I think she only wished she'd had the same experience with her mother, but the times were different and it was what she missed out in her relationship with her mother that drove her to make the effort to make our relationship what it was.

Being without her has been an adjustment to say the least. She would be so proud of my brother and me and the relationship that we had with our father for the five years, until his sudden departure from our lives recently (September 19, 2013). I think of her every day and I miss her and I know that will never change! This strong and flavourful taste of paprika will stay with us forever.

Marika and Vicky

Mark and Marika

MY MOTHER
Mark Ainley

A scientist who loved to organize and understand, my mother herself defied categorization. She was a force of nature (no wonder she liked to spend so much time in it). Her curiosity was contagious and she fostered investigation all around her. An admired professor with multi-disciplinary interests, she always sought to learn new things, meet new people, and explore new vistas.

Her support of exploration began at home and she shared that with her family. As a child with a scientific bent, I studied multiple disciplines with her encouragement. When I was still in my early elementary school years, she took me to a university laboratory so I could try running a mouse through a maze I had built, also explaining the myriad beakers of mysterious looking fluids in the lab. She would help me find carnivorous plants in the wild and encouraged my writing, helping me get my first official publication on the topic in a dedicated newsletter at the age of 14.

It is little surprise that she was drawn to chemistry. She herself was a unique blend, rather fiery, occasionally volatile, who mixed well with some kinds (but not all) and could certainly enjoy the occasional alcohol solution. It would be inaccurate to say she was a catalyst - one who brought about change in others while remaining unchanged because, while she did indeed help others achieve their potential, that was something that ennobled and changed her too.

She was as comfortable gleaning the wisdom from her forebears as she was in encouraging her students. I recall meeting with her two amazing women who inspired her tremendously. We visited the lovely Louise de Kiriline Lawrence in her log cabin off RR1 in Ontario, and my mother expressed such gratitude and admiration for her while listening with rapt attention. On another occasion we visited Doris Speirs in her home in a similar setting. Speirs had been friends with the Group of Seven, and when we entered the smaller cabin at the back of the property, we saw the floor was lined with stacks of private paintings by the famous artists, stacked three deep. The collection went to the National Gallery in Ottawa when Spears died; my mother and I had always hoped we'd inherit a Lawren Harris.

She was at once down-to-earth and appreciative of the finer things in life. She wasn't always fussed about the more delicate side of cooking: she prepared delectable roast beef with Yorkshire pudding, but could just as easily whip up a mean jambalaya or throw together some hot dogs & fries or macaroni & cheese. But she had standards for the dining table no matter what the meal: there would never be a plastic container visible, as all drinks would be in decanters, all spreads and condiments in pewter dishes or silver trays. The respect and dignity she sought to embody personally translated to the presentation of the dining area.

Someone who saw far beyond the surface, she nevertheless liked to present herself well. She loved to dress up for concerts and parties (she couldn't understand how people could go to a classical concert in jeans), but was equally at ease birdwatching in boots, jeans, and a parka. For her, being a feminist was not antithetical to embracing her femininity and enhancing her appearance. I'll never forget that when she woke up from surgery, in a half daze, she said, "Oh good, you're here... Where's my lipstick?" and then went on to apply it with absolute precision, without a mirror.

Our relationship evolved significantly over the course of my life, and she went from being a guiding light to one who also asked for advice and respected my opinion. In my late teens, she asked me to proofread her writing because she admired my sense of composition and use of grammar. In her second phase of her final illness, with less energy than usual, she phoned one day distraught at not being able to do as much as she'd like and asked what I thought she might do. I suggested even a short outing to a different coffee shop than usual while also taking a different route than she might ordinarily, so that it all felt new. She did so and phoned back thrilled that her adventurousness felt stimulated again. While always up for something big, she could delight at the simplest things.

Such was her vivacious energy and youthful appearance that many people had no idea she was sick. She still looked great, painted with the Madrona group in Victoria, went for walks, and met with friends. She had to rest more at home but enjoyed doing what she could. She still spent lots of time on the phone with friends all over the world, as well as with her family. When she finally entered hospital after a severe chemo session, she came to peace with the fact that she was on her way out. "I'm not afraid of dying. It's not what everyone thinks," she said.

She wanted there to be a Celebration of Life in her memory that was truly celebratory. Friends and relatives from all over the country attended a lively, upbeat afternoon in Victoria that honoured her many attributes and dimensions. (Other celebrations were held in Montreal and Prince George; the flags flew at half mast at the University of Northern British Columbia in PG.) On the way to the first party in Victoria, my sister and I spotted a bald eagle flying ahead of us that seemed to be guiding the way. When we entered the room, Mum's painting of a bald eagle flying head-on out of the canvas was directly in front of us. Since that day, we have considered it to be her totem. Other than her beloved owl, there couldn't be a better symbol to represent her: noble, majestic, with a far-reaching overview of a wide expanse, respected as a leader and admired for her beauty.

Marika in Montreal, Q.C., 1960s

MY FATHER
Mark Ainley

In my father, David Ainley, my mother found a staunch ally and supporter. They not only shared a great love for each other but were well-matched on numerous levels - a love of nature, an interest in music and literature, a sharp wit, and rather acidic tongue - and my father's help with my mother's work was immeasurable. He took on extra work in order to help support the family while she pursued her higher education. He read every word she wrote and she said he was the best editor she ever had. He drove us all across the continent numerous times, our family trips integrating her research and bird-watching explorations. In later years, he joined her on international voyages that incorporated her work projects. They were true partners in life, and all that my mother accomplished was supported by my father. No tribute to her would be complete without appreciation for all that he did for her.

David Ainley, age 72, Western Australia, near Perth, 2006.

A TOAST TO MARIKA
David Ainley

Marika was born in Budapest on December 4, 1937 to Martin and Sara Gosztonyi. She was loved and cherished from the beginning, and had the advantages of an upper-middle class upbringing for a while. All too soon, life was disrupted by World War II. Life became quite difficult, and when Gyöngyi was born on September 16, 1942, the operating room lights went out due to an air raid. They survived the war and its various trials and tribulations, and eventually the Russians fought it out with the fascists in Budapest, and one result was the destruction of Martin Gosztonyi's office. For a few years, some semblance of normalcy returned. Although gifted intellectually, Marika detested school during this period. Being very intelligent she was totally bored in large classes doing rote learning. Conformity was never her style.

The next major event in Marika's life was the 1956 Hungarian uprising. She thought, "NO, not again!" At nineteen, she and some others were escorted over the Hungarian border at night with a guide who was able to succeed in avoiding military patrols wanting to stop this type of activity.

She was delighted to leave Hungary to stay nine months in Stockholm with her father's brother Charles, who was a very successful violinist and had three children of his own. It was at this time that a family Swedish connection was established which has endured to this day. After that, it was on to Montreal and, eventually, one big winner was yours truly! We met on March 14, 1964 at a Welsh party that we both came close to missing. Fortunately we went and it was essentially a case of "Lust at first sight."

After that life became complicated and interesting for a while, as we were both already married and Marika had a daughter, Vicky. In the summer of 1964, we set off from Montreal in a 1958 Chevrolet on a three-and-a-half-week, 9000-mile driving holiday: Montreal, Winnipeg, Banff, Vancouver, Seattle, San Francisco, Yosemite, Nevada, Chicago, Niagara Falls, and Montreal. We had one Texaco credit card, spent $27.00 on accommodation including one-night hotel stays in San Francisco, Chicago, and the mid-west. In Chicago we saw Oscar Peterson and his trio at the London House. For $2.50 each, we sat ten feet away from him and each had a B&B – quite amazing and unforgettable.

What did I learn on this trip? That Marika was easy to talk to and had a wonderful sense of humour, that she was an intellectual, and that when she was hungry, you got her and food together at the very first opportunity and not thirty miles down the highway. She was into archeology at this point and walked on mountain slopes looking down for Indian arrowheads, unsuccessfully. One of her many talents was to go into our antiquated tent wearing jeans or shorts and come out ten minutes later looking like a fashion queen. She looked fantastic if we stayed in the tent too! It became quite clear that we wanted to spend our lives together. Eventually, after some difficulties and challenging legal proceedings courtesy of Quebec, we were married in Montreal on July 23, 1966 and did just that.

Marika's next interests were birding and pottery. Birding became an obsession and typically she was not simply a twitcher (a lister), but took an advanced correspondence course in ornithology offered by Cornell University. She quickly became a hot-shot authority on birding.

On November 26, 1969, Mark arrived early in the morning, much to Vicky's chagrin. He, too, was loved and cherished, and with Vicky to translate his weird sounds, did not speak coherently until he was two and a half when in the Laurentians, north of Montreal, he said, "Shut up, you stupid Jays." Indeed they were very noisy at the time. Our next cross-Canada trip saw Marika trying to look up for birds and down for artifacts at the same time. Birds won out. By this time, we were really organized, well-equipped campers, with good tents and clothing, and two Coleman stoves for cooking excellent meals.

After I got an M.A. and a pay raise, Marika went back to the University of Montreal and took an M.A. in History of Science (in French, her third language), and then continued her History of Science studies at McGill, taking a Ph.D.

Eventually she was appointed Principal of Simone de Beauvoir Institute of Women's Studies at Concordia University. This was when her academic influence and feminist interests really expanded and she was able to help a lot of people. However, it was a demanding job and she had to deal with some difficult personalities and dynamics. At one tense meeting, with motions flying around all over the place, she exclaimed, "I'm getting motion sickness". As could be expected, this defused the situation.

When I retired from teaching at the end of 1994, Marika obtained a job to be the first Chair of Women's Studies at UNBC starting in 1995. We were glad to be out of Quebec, just before Parizeau's referendum, and in Prince George, British Columbia, with its wonderfully kind and caring community. Once again, though, Marika had difficult dynamics to contend with at UNBC. She could and did help many people, and to help herself, she took up painting with the energy, enthusiasm, and ability that she brought to all her pursuits.

We were in Victoria for only four and a half years, and people here might not realize how we both formerly had a lot more energy in Prince George. Marika quickly made, as always, many friends in different areas of life and additionally became part of a wonderful painting group, The Madronas, here at the Goward House, where she requested to have this celebration of her life. She was always very happy painting here with a wonderful group of women in a beautiful natural setting.

Over the years, we had many holiday trips, camping in the east and west, and also visiting Europe, and Sweden in particular. We also made four trips to Australia, two to New Zealand, and one to Fiji. Our last holiday, which rivaled the success of our first one, was a two week Alaskan Cruise which we both enjoyed enormously. Marika was seemingly fit, enthusiastic as always, and looked fantastic.

A few weeks after our return, she was admitted to hospital. During her last days, she still ran the show, indicating where paintings, cards, and pictures should be placed. She talked beyond her strength, but as always communicated superbly. Mercifully, her intellectual ability remained, and it is worth mentioning that she had an in-depth knowledge of archeology, anthropology, ornithology, philosophy, chemistry, literature, languages, pottery, painting, classical music, opera, jazz, and photography. She was a true pantheist and loved nature to the fullest.

In her final days, tributes and comments poured in and some of these comments were repeated: "zest for life", "caring", "sympathetic", "encouraging", "inspiring", "vibrant nature," "vivacious". She had the same restless energy as did William Rowan, about whom she wrote a biography with that title. Perhaps one day, someone will write a book on Marika's life. It would be a rich topic with no shortage of subject matter in many areas.

At this point, I would like to propose a toast to Marika.

You made a difference living life to the fullest.

You did it your way, and your way was fantastic.

Thank you for everything.

Well done, Marika! Thank you!

Marika and David on the Alaska cruise, August 2008

MY ONLY SISTER
Gyöngyi Belfer

My sister and I were born about 5 years apart, she just before the war and I in the middle of it. She wasn't particularly thrilled when I arrived - she made a comment about wanting to throw me out the window... she didn't want the competition for our parents' affection. Like many children, we had rivalries that we would eventually grow out of. My introduction to school was being asked if I was smart like my sister was - but I was not interested in competing with her. She used to hide under the bed to read her books so she could avoid doing housework. Once when our parents went out of town and left us money for food, she talked me into buying opera records instead of going out to dinner. But I could be a brat when we were young too: when she had her boyfriends over and wanted the lights off, I would turn them on.

She escaped during the Hungarian Revolution in 1956, and my parents and I followed her to Sweden in 1957. She didn't stay long, though, and she left for Canada. I went to Montreal to visit her in 1962 and I decided to stay. She was having a difficult time when her marriage with George wasn't going well, but things certainly improved when she met David.

We were 5 years apart, but as we got older it became 4 and 3/4. We didn't get along particularly well as kids because of the age difference, but as time went on we became the best of friends. We respected each other. We could talk about anything and everything. We spoke to each other several times a day, when living in the same city and also after she had moved across the country. We appreciated each others' qualities more and in our later years we had painting in common. It was a real pleasure when she visited me in Montreal and came to my studio - we had a wonderful time as she sat down with us and enjoyed our time painting together.

When I was turning 65 I didn't want a party but she talked me into it (she was good at that), and she and David came back to Montreal to celebrate. I am so glad that we had that happy time together. She looked beautiful, made a wonderful speech, and we have many great photos of the occasion. It was not long afterwards that she got sick.

When I went to visit her in her final weeks, she said that the doctors had given her less than two months to live. But she said that she had told

David that the following summer we'd all rent a big place and the whole family would come together to visit. She loved our family as her own - she was a great aunt to my children, and she loved my grandchildren as if they were her own, and they all adored her... the grandkids always wanted to sit beside her when she visited and they loved spending time with her.

I still miss her terribly. I still want to pick up the phone to call her to discuss things with her. I see her photo every day. I know there are so many people who respected her and loved her. I am grateful that I had her in my life for as long as I did, although she was taken from us too soon.

Marika and Gyöngyi

NO DAYS WITHOUT LAUGHTER
Louis Gosztonyi

They say first impressions last. Indeed it was so in this case. The year was 1948 and I was just four years old and my parents, my two older sisters and I had just arrived in Budapest after two days or more on the train from Stockholm. Now it was time to go to Hungary to visit our family there for the first time after World War II. Now it was safe going by train again in central Europe.

From the ferry boat between Trelleborg and Sassnitz there were ship wrecks at the horizon. They looked just like toys to me but my sister Manci, who was six, became anxious. Mum, Dad and Franci were trying to comfort her.

The harbour in Sassnitz, Poland, was just a lot of bricks and rubbish everywhere, and along the railroad in Poland here and there you could see skeletons half concealed by sand or the remains of clothes. My oldest sister Franci covered my eyes.

In Czechoslovakia, or maybe it was in Slovakia, I only remembered sitting on the table in the coupé singing. The window was open and at a small station people were applauding me.

In Budapest my uncle's family lived ten minutes' walk from the West-bahnhof. The train station was huge. I liked the smell of steam.

The entrance of the building where my cousins lived was impressive. There were granite banisters and a sofa and the steps were larger than any I'd ever climbed before. We went up the lift. Oh how I loved taking lifts! Really smart! When going upwards (I don't know how high it was, maybe three or four floors), sounds emerged, like birds. High shrill, giggles and screams increased the higher the lift climbed. Higher and higher. Then the doors opened and there they were; Marika and Gyöngyi, my cousins. I had older Hungarian cousins too.

My Hungarian cousins! We were the only ones I knew of having Hungarian cousins!

There were some extra stairs before we reached their doorstep. Then there were lots of hugs and kisses for everybody. I got my share and it was a great deal. Being the little brother, most of them sort of landed on me, on my forehead and hair. They seemed to like my red hair! Even my freckles! And how they could smile, Marika and Gyöngyi! We smiled a lot in my family, especially me, but here were even more smiles.

Their smiles made a great impression on me. Every time in life we met after that there were all those smiles. They really knew how to smile, no matter where or when. When we were talking of our fathers and mothers gone long time ago, we were smiling. Marika had many talents. One of them was making people smile, not only me of course, but me very much.

We didn't see each other very often in our lives. Canada and Sweden are, as everybody knows, not close at all – but Marika and I were.

It was absolutely a genetic thing – the making me smile. Genes count. In our lives we lived under the same roof maybe four or five months at the most, always with a smile. Not one day went by without laughing. And no phone call ever took place without lots of joking and laughing. That has been the case, since day one, in 1948.

Marika, Louis Gosztonyi (cousin), and Jan Ulrik Tullberg (cousin Manci's husband)

MY DEAREST AINLEYS
Stina, Jonas, Ebba and Melker

We are so sorry that we could not attend the celebration of your wonderful Marika today. But that does not mean that our thoughts are not with you. On the contrary, we are with you all this day, and all other days. Be strong, be brave, but also let go. Hopefully she is in a better place with no more pain, and we will meet her again someday. Maybe this life is just a passage on to the next level. Who knows.

We raise our glasses in one last toast.

Hear Hear this is to you Marika!

So many thoughts pass by, memories of you that keep us warm inside, like a nice woolen blanket on a cold winter's day. At the same time, it hurts badly inside, knowing that we will not be able to see you once again. Ebba still speaks of you, remembering the funny aunt and uncle who spoke in a funny language and who played with her in our apartment at Lilla Essingen. When I told her that you were ill, she wanted us to go and visit you. We will miss you terribly, and I hope that you feel our love for you, even though we are far away.

Go peacefully, and remember, you will always be in our hearts. We love you.

Marika, Vicky, Mark, David, early 1970s

Marika with her parents

Marika and Gyöngyi

Marika, Montreal, 1960s

Marika and Gyöngyi

Marika in Montreal

Facing Mt. Baker

Friends and Colleagues

CELEBRATION OF MARIKA'S LIFE – OCTOBER 18, 2008
GOWARD HOUSE, VICTORIA, B.C.,
Mary E. Baldwin

Marika, or Marianne as she introduced herself to me when we first met, is one of my oldest and dearest friends in Canada. We met in the fall of 1966 in the Chemistry Department at Loyola College in Montreal. She had just begun working for Dr. Nogrady, a fellow Hungarian, as a research assistant, and I had just started working as a laboratory instructor supervising organic chemistry labs. Loyola at that time was a Jesuit run four-year college for men, and there were very few women who were not secretaries or office staff. We shared the problems of being isolated professional women in science, working mothers with young children. (Vicky is between my daughters in age.) We were both immigrants, and had experienced discrimination against married women in the workplace, and the problems of qualifications from another country, although we came from very different places. I came from Tasmania, while she left Hungary following the 1956 uprising, after completing a Diploma of Industrial Chemistry at the Polytechnical College of Chemistry in Budapest. She had worked in laboratories in Montreal while completing her B.A. at night school at what was then Sir George Williams University (now Concordia), with concentrations in English and French literature.

There were many upheavals and changes in the political and educational scene in Montreal during the late 60's, and as time passed and our children grew, she became increasingly frustrated with the role of research assistant, where one's contribution to a project may be substantial but the principal investigator receives the recognition—and one may not be able to pursue good research ideas.

She was interested in anthropology and had applied and been accepted into a master's program when life intervened in 1969 in the form of Mark. She had introduced me to espresso coffee, and regularly made espresso in a little pressure machine in the basement kitchen, and quite suddenly she went off espresso coffee. I was not surprised when she finally admitted she was pregnant.

So graduate school was put on hold, and she was at home while Mark was a young child. During this time she found creative outlets through pottery and her passion for birding. I still have some of her hand-made pots, when she was experimenting with form and glazes. She actively pursued her interest in birding, a lifelong passion, and completed Cornell University's Certificate in Ornithology in 1979.

Marika returned to work at Loyola in 1974, first as a research assistant and then as a laboratory instructor for General Chemistry, but did not give up on the notion of graduate school. Although our careers took different paths, and I remained at Loyola then Concordia, we neither of us wanted to become "Mrs. Godblesshers" referred to in Vivian Gornick's book on Women in Science, content to mind laboratories for years. A chemistry colleague Michael Hogben who was involved in Interdisciplinary Studies at Loyola at the time suggested she check out the History of Science program at Université de Montréal. She had found her field, and enrolled in the Institut d'histoire et de politique des sciences, where she was able to combine her interest in the scientific contributions of amateurs and her love of ornithology, completing an M.Sc in 1980: *La professionalisation de l'ornithologie Amricaine 1870 –1979*. This was tough, and a real triumph, as much of the reading and seminars were in French, (a third language) and all theses at Université de Montréal must satisfy their language watchdog before submission, but this experience enhanced her French/English bilingualism. She was hooked on research, received a doctoral fellowship, and moved to McGill for her Ph.D in the History and Philosophy of Science program, expanding on the work she had begun in ornithology, on professionalisation of this field science, the role and contributions of amateurs, and issues of colonialism and science, receiving her degree in 1985 for her thesis *From Natural History to Avian Biology: Canadian Ornithology 1860-1950*.

The work for her graduate degrees required extensive archival research across Canada, and interviewing those involved in ornithology who were still alive and their descendants for insights and information. These field trips for research were combined with the family summer camping holidays. David was then teaching high school in the PSBGM, and this pattern of travel and research has continued across the years – summer camping trips and travel destinations built around visits to archives and libraries and interviews with people relevant to the current research project across Canada, in the US, and on trips to UK, Sweden , and more recently sabbatical leaves in Australia and New Zealand.

In 1985 she received a research grant from Social Sciences & Humanities Research Council's (SSHRC) as an independent researcher to work on a scientific biography of William Rowan, a British trained ornithologist who came to Canada to establish the Zoology Department at the University of Alberta. She had become very interested in his experimental work on bird migration and the problems he encountered as a field researcher in the course of her doctoral research, and writing his scientific biography was a project dear to her heart.

However, research grants do not provide income to the individual, and there was a dearth of academic positions available in the 80's. It was also very difficult at that time (before email and the internet) to be an independent researcher without an institutional affiliation to provide a base, access to libraries and archives, colleagues for discussion and collaboration, etc. She did complete the biography *Restless Energy - A Biography of William Rowan, 1891-1957,* which was published with a SSHRC publication grant in 1993.

Meanwhile a change of direction in her research interests took place. Marika and I regularly walked and talked in Hampstead, a mazelike suburb of Montreal, near where she lived; I always got lost, but she knew every bird likely to be spotted en route. On one of these walks we realized that there was potential money for research in Canadian Women and Science under the umbrella of SSHRC's new Women and Work program, and that she was eminently qualified to apply for it. Margaret Rossiter's book on American (meaning US) Women Scientists had come out in 1982, but there was little historical information about Canadian women natural scientists at that time, although she had come across women naturalists in her graduate work. She received a SSHRC PDF in 85-86 to work on History of Canadian Women in Science, which she spent in the History Department at McGill, and in 1986 obtained the first of two SSHRC major strategic grants covering 1986-92 for Women and Scientific Work, as an Independent Scholar. She still wanted an institutional affiliation and I introduced her to Arpi Hamalian, the Principal of the Simone de Beauvoir Institute at Concordia University, who suggested that she become a Research Fellow of the Institute, which was the start of her association with the Institute.

Women and Scientific Work in Canada has been one of the main themes of her research, which has branched in many directions, including oral histories of living Canadian women scientists, archival work on earlier women scientists, their lives and struggles, interviews with their descendants, and examining how they pursued their scientific interests despite barriers. More recently her work has expanded to women and the environment and issues related to the transfer and recognition of First Nations environmental knowledge, and the cultural parallels between the Australian, New Zealand and Canadian experience, all having been former British colonies.

In 1988 she began teaching part-time in the Women's Studies program at the Simone de Beauvoir, developing a course in Historical and Contemporary Perspectives of Women, Science and Technology. On one of our walks when discussing the problems she encountered in finding reading material for her course, asking for preprints of papers and conference presentations from colleagues working in this area in Canada, I suggested the solution was for her to create a book. So she solicited a series of essays, which she edited and "Despite the Odds: Essays on Canadian Women and Science" (Véhicule Press) was published in 1990.

She spent a year at Carlton University as Visiting Scholar in their Women's Studies program then in 1991 became Principal of the Simone de Beauvoir and Director of the Women's Studies program for the next four years. During this time she provided dynamic leadership to the Institute, introducing innovations in the curriculum and teaching methods, actively encouraging research seminars and fostering collaborations with colleagues in other departments. She herself was actively involved in collaborations with colleagues on oral histories, feminist research methods, and feminist biography. She also gained experience in academic administration.

In 1995 the opportunity to become Professor and Chair of Women's Studies at the new UNBC in Prince George provided a fresh challenge and a secure tenured academic position. It was a major move, supported by David, who was able to take retirement from the school system where he had taught for more than 30 years. At UNBC she had the opportunity to shape and teach in their Women's Studies program, develop a graduate program, and supervise graduate students. She loved teaching and working with her graduate students on their research projects. Her teaching received external recognition with the Teaching as if the World Mattered Award in 2001 in Toronto from the Biology as if the World Mattered Research Group. Her outstanding contribution to UNBC has been recognized when she was made Professor Emerita, at a special ceremony there in 2005. Following her mandatory retirement in 2002, she and David moved to Victoria where she actively continued her research and writing projects, and developed as an artist. (She had started to paint as a creative outlet while in Prince George, and painted regularly in Victoria with the Madrona group of women artists.)

Marika was a highly productive and well-funded scholar recognized in her fields by her peers. She was elected for three terms as President of the Canadian Science and Technology Historical Association, from 1993-1999, and President of the Women's Studies Association 1999-2000. In addition to her own books, she has contributed more than 20 book chapters to other collections, written numerous peer reviewed journal articles, made contributions to Oxford Companion to Canadian History, the Biographical Dictionary of North American environmentalists, the New Oxford Dictionary of National Biography, as well as writing many reviews of books in history of science, women and science, and ornithology, and serving as a consultant to several museums and Science Centres.

She believed in sharing the ideas and insights which she developed, and as well as regular conference presentations. For the past twenty years she has been an invited speaker several times a year to a wide range of disciplinary and interdisciplinary gatherings.

There were always multiple projects on the go, and most recently, despite her illness, since retirement she had finally completed and submitted for publication the book synthesizing years of her historical work on Canadian women scientists in academia. Late this summer she received the first reviews of the manuscript *Overlooked Dimensions: Women and Scientific Work at Canadian Universities 1884-1980,* suggesting some revisions late this summer, but sadly she was not able to complete them. It is my hope that her book will be published, and this valuable work not lost.

Marika's path from research assistant in chemistry to eminent scholar in History of Science and Women's Studies would not have been possible without the love and support of David and her children, Vicky and Mark. David's Yorkshire skepticism, dry wit and endless patience kept her grounded, and provided encouragement through all the difficult times and frustrations. He has driven countless miles over the years enabling her research on a shoestring while sharing her love of nature and photographing birds. He has been, she always told me, the best editor of her writings, ensuring clarity and clear use of language. If David did not understand, the text needed change.

For me, Marika has been a wonderful, vibrant, warm and colorful friend, who has given me support and encouragement for more than forty years. She left us too soon, but has touched the lives of all her many friends and colleagues who are gathered here today for this celebration. She has given us all so much, and her life has had a ripple effect on our lives. For me, the titles of her books in many ways reflect her life. She herself was full of restless energy, and her career is an example of what can be accomplished in scholarship and creativity despite the odds.

Marika graduating from McGill with her Ph.D., 1985

A CELEBRATION OF MARIKA
LOYOLA CHAPEL, CONCORDIA UNIVERSITY, NOVEMBER 9, 2008
Susan Hoecker-Drysdale

On the afternoon of October 18, 2008, at the Goward House, a senior activity and art center in Victoria, BC, approximately eighty-five people came together to celebrate the life of Marika Gosztonyi Ainley. The gathering was warm and animated as the attendees exchanged stories about Marika and spoke of their relationships and experiences with her. Indeed, the gloom and sorrow normally attending such occasions were overpowered by remembrances filled with joy and the jubilance that human beings feel when sharing a strong personal life connection. The chattering, consuming of superb hors-d'oeuvres, and toasting Marika went on for an hour and half at least, and then we paused for tributes. David Ainley began with an exquisite and beautifully presented account of Marika's life and of their lives together. He was followed by Marika's sister Gyongyi's heartfelt description of their lives as sisters. Mary Baldwin presented a comprehensive and personal account that only she could compose, about Marika's academic life and the ways in which they shared the challenging experiences of careers with family responsibilities. Finally, Annelie Dominik, an artist friend and fellow member of the Madrona Studio, poignantly described and analyzed Marika's artistic work in all its complexities and beauty, to the delight of everyone present. The room was filled with some of Marika's paintings and artifacts, including a recent portrait of Marika and a video of photos taken over many years. Upstairs the Madrona Group's fall exhibition, dedicated to Marika, filled several rooms, including one entire room to honour Marika's art.

I knew that you would want to know about that commemoration in Victoria; it was an afternoon to be savoured, a celebration of Marika's life, exactly what she had requested. No mournful and lengthy funeral for her! This was a true reflection of Marika. The event reflected very much her years in British Columbia and the many friends she and David made there—colleagues and students at UNBC, members of the Prince George and Victoria communities, the women of the Madrona Art Studio, members of the Hungarian Society of Victoria, colleagues at The University of Victoria, the doctor from the Hospice (by the way, a Yorkshireman), members of the Retired Women Historians group, retired Montrealers and indeed, Concordia faculty who now live in Victoria, and so on.

But aside from all of this, that occasion, and this commemoration today, are indicative of Marika's life, her place in the world and her impact upon the lives of all who knew her. For, along with all her intellectual, scientific, artistic, and naturalist interests and her talents, Marika's interests in and concern for others—including students, colleagues, artists, community members, friends and friends of friends, members of the Hungarian community, the Native Canadian community, birders and naturalists, and those she encountered in her scholarly and artistic activities and daily life—seemed infinite and spanned a continent. To know Marika was to be her friend. She didn't always agree with you; indeed she was of an independent mind, but she cared about you. The key to friendship is honesty, acceptance, and empathy, all of which Marika had in abundance.

She and we were devastated at the diagnosis of breast cancer a few years ago. But she weathered that storm, met the challenge straight on, and continued her life, almost uninterrupted. She expressed her own feelings and fears, as well as her joys and hopes, in her art and in conversation. One of her many gifts to her friends was advice—advice to live life to its fullest, to be determined to get through the "rough stuff" that inevitably comes along, to "never give up", to take advantage of opportunities to see the world, especially the natural world, in all its splendor, to establish friendships and remain in touch with and faithful to friends, to develop one's own talents and interests without delay, to have the courage to do something new, to challenge yourself, to love those around you, to reach out to those who need friendship and love, to support each other "in sickness and in health", and to consider your priorities in life and forget about the obstacles or problems. She touched us all, and she is a significant part of us. In various ways, she brought us all together.

I have known Marika for many years, since Mary Baldwin introduced us at a meeting at McGill in the 1970s. We have been close friends for almost that long and grew increasingly closer during her last years in Montreal and since. Our friendship was nurtured by phone calls and emails. We spoke on the phone every day and talked about professional and personal matters, our families, our concerns, and about the details of, and our own reactions to, our shared battles with cancer. We published together and participated in professional meetings which included trips to New Orleans, Santa Fe, PEI and elsewhere, went birding, to which she had introduced me, took many walks around NDG, Hampstead and

Westmount Summit, shared our feminist interests within and outside of the Simone de Beauvoir Institute, and enjoyed parties and dinners with and without our husbands. The days seem empty without those telephone conversations, but every time I see a bird, a beautiful tree or flower or sunset, I think of her. Marika would not leave us in sadness, regret or heartache. She wants us to celebrate life, celebrate our friendships, our time together, celebrate our personal self-actualization and that of others, and celebrate nature, especially birds, rocks, flowers and plants of all sorts, sunsets and phases of the moon, all that makes our existence meaningful and worthwhile. If we do, she will laugh and lift a glass to us, and be pleased.

Marika and Susan Hoecker-Drysdale, Victoria, B.C. June 2008

A CELEBRATION OF THE LIFE OF MARIKA AINLEY
Barbara Meadowcroft

The last strains of the music died away. We were gathered in the Loyola Chapel to celebrate Marika's life. I had chosen the music for a special reason. It was the final movement of Beethoven's sixth symphony. Earlier that year the CBC had had a Beethoven Festival. They asked listeners to write in with their Beethoven stories. Marika evoked the winter of 1970-71, which was then the record for the most snowfall in Montreal's history. The sidewalks of NDG (Notre Dame de Grace) were choked with snow, impassable for a stroller. Marika was confined to the house with an overactive toddler. David would dash home, grab a bite, and dash out again (he was teaching for the Protestant School Board, teenagers during the day, adults at night) leaving Marika to put the kids to bed and stand at the window watching the snow pile up. Then she heard that Beethoven's nine symphonies were being offered on special. They borrowed the money, (things were tight now that Marika was not working) and rushed off to buy a set. "After we bought the LP set," she said, "I still spent time watching the snow flakes, but listening to the symphonies, I felt hope return and my spirit soared with the music. I knew then that spring would come. Beethoven saved my sanity, if not my life."

I first met Marika on a field trip with the PQSPB (Province of Quebec Society for the Protection of Birds). Nancy Schumann, a relatively new birder herself, introduced us. Marika asked me what I was doing. I reeled off a list of things, knowing it sounded unimpressive for someone with a Ph.D. "You should join the Simone de Beauvoir Institute," she said. That was in 1988. Twenty years later and I was still there, then the longest serving Research Associate at the Institute. Marika took my academic career in hand. When she was editing *Despite the Odds*, she told me she needed an article on Alice Wilson, the first Canadian professional geologist. "What do I know about geology?" I said. She told me that she would give me some notes she had and I could expand upon them. That was Marika—always generous with her own research, eager to help others up the academic ladder. Thanks to her I got my first publication. When my book *Painting Friends* came out, Marika, who was Director of Women's Studies at University of Northern BC, insisted that I come to Prince George. "Apply for a grant," she said. So I did. The Canada

Council gave me a travel grant to introduce the work of Canadian women painters to the west. I went to Calgary, Vancouver, and Victoria; but I started out in Prince George.

Marika was always very concerned with her friends' health. When I fractured my hip on an icy Montreal pavement, she immediately mobilized her network. All day I lay in the ward waiting for my operation. About six-thirty I was finally taken to the operating room. A gowned figure stepped forward, lowered his mask, and said "Hullo, Barbara. The other fellow had been operating all day. I sent him home and I'm going to operate on your hip."

"I know you," I said. "You're a birder."

"I'm also a damn good surgeon," he replied.

It was Dr. Ross Murphy.

Marika was always planning something new. After retirement, and the move to Victoria, she and David went to Australia. She was interested in Aboriginal women and their overlooked contributions to science. It was a shock to hear that she was ill, and then two years later that the cancer had returned. I was full of admiration for the way she handled her illness. No self-pity. Aquafit three times a week, more hours of painting (she had taken it up while at UNBC to dispel the stress), and a renewed effort to finish her book on women scientists in Canadian Universities. In August she phoned. Her voice sounded tired, broken. They were going to try one last chemo. Then it was Vicky telling me that her mother was in the hospice and not to phone but to consult the blog that Mark had set up. Two weeks later Vicky called again.

"She wants to speak to you," she said and gave me the phone number. I dialled the hospice.

"I'm coming out," I said.

"When?"

I thought quickly. "This week. Friday."

"Oh, no. That's much too soon. Come the next weekend. The art exhibit will be on. We'll have more fun." That was Marika; even then she was looking ahead.

"No, I said, "I'm coming now." Three days later I was on the plane.

Her room at the hospice was filled with cards and paintings. Vicky had brushed her mother's hair and put a many-coloured wrap around her shoulders. Even so, the change was shocking. We exchanged a few words. She was well enough to write some phone numbers for me. She wanted me to meet her painting friends, who were organizing an exhibition. By the next day she had fallen into a deep sleep. Her painting of houses at Robin's Hood Bay still glowed in her window, but her spirit did not.

Rai Brown, Marika, Anne-Marie Weidler Kubanek, Barbara Meadowcroft. Midsummer night celebration at Sommerøya outside Tromsø, Norway, 1999.

MARIKA
Nancy Schumann

Hanging on my wall is a small watercolor Marika did of Osoyoos, BC, called "Windy Day," painted in 1997 toward the beginning of her active interest in painting. Blowing trees are framed by a brownish gray mountain; in the sky overhead, two gulls are flying. Marika gave this to me as a gift, and it is, indeed, a gift because of what it means to me. Marika went on to develop her painting skills to a very high level. Later, I purchased a picture she painted of Ayers Rock, a study in shades of rust and orange, which I sent to my nephew in San Francisco. She painted with great intensity, great interest, and great love, so much like the person she is.

All who knew Marika know of her many talents. My remembrance is one of her as a friend. We became friends on a birding trip in the early 1980s with the PQSPB; she encouraged me to continue my birding. Her lively wit, enthusiasm, and her caring for nature and for people, captured my heart. Over the years I enjoyed getting to know David, Vicky, Mark, her mother, and Gyongyi and many of her friends from near and far. We both left Montreal, yet our friendship continued to flourish. It was exciting to visit her in Prince George, BC, and then later in Victoria. She continued to grow, to learn, and to blossom.

I feel so much richer having known Marika. She encouraged me to "Just Be You!" I cherish her small painting, a reminder of her grace and of her unique ability to accept and to be herself without any apologies and without self-importance.

MARIKA
Kenneth W. Thorpe

My intense involvement over several years with the bird society (PQSPB – now BPQ) was a result of Marika taking me under her "wing." She befriended and mentored me, an aspiring birder, about 1977 and soon had me on the bird society board where I served for many years, including "stints" as treasurer and president. I often picked her up and drove her off to weekly PQSPB field trips and got to know her family, especially her husband David. (Stints are also Eurasian shorebirds.)

Ironically, when reading a current ABA Birding magazine, I noted an interview with a prominent ornithologist named David Ainley. Who knew? Actually David was mildly interested in birdlife, and well tolerated Marika's passion for things avian. I can still hear him saying "Yes, love" in reference to almost anything in his soft British accent.

When Marika heard I was planning a camping trip to the Canadian Rockies, she made sure she told me where I could find several bird species. "You must go to Johnson Canyon to look for Dippers," she proclaimed and indeed we went to Johnson Canyon in Banff National Park and indeed there was the Dipper, walking around the fast flowing water, over rocks and under cascades looking for invertebrate snacks that were then fed to its wing-wagging fledgling. That and a few other western birds were my first sightings and proudly added to my Life List. Thanks, Marika.

Marika was a natural choice for the editorial committee for the 1982 PQSPB 75th anniversary book on the organization's history. Given her passion for history of science and particularly the history of Canadian ornithology there were always new explorations to be done and the project took somewhat longer than expected. I had never gotten around to reading *A Bird in the Bush*, but recently did and, by chance also re-established contact with the author, Margaret Pye Arnaudin, herself a long time birder and friend of Marika's. Margaret reminisced about working with Marika and how there was always another path of exploration to go down, always one more person to interview.

Marika's biography of William Rowan, *Restless Energy*, is inscribed to Ken, Janice and Jonathan, September 1993. Janice and I met while we were both on the PQSPB board, and indeed after marriage along came

Jonathan in 1992. Janice fondly remembers that Marika befriended her and her parents on field trips and without Marika"s encouragement, she would not have become a volunteer newsletter copy preparer and eventually a board member. So Marika`s befriending us both made a rather significant contribution to our lives together.

In my copy of *Restless Energy* is also the program from *A Celebration of the Life of Dr. Marianne (Marika) Gosztonyi Ainley,* November 9, 2008. I spoke at that service on "Marika as an enthusiastic birder" and shared some birding memories. I did not keep my notes and spoke extemporaneously but did make a comment to the effect that Marika was not always the easiest person to get along with. The attendees chuckled. Indeed she was critical, often argumentative but always with a purpose. And she was warm and kind and she was a friend.

Marika birding at the home of Carl von Linnés's home "Hammarby" in Sweden, where in 1753, Linnés published "Species Plantarum." Linnés simplified the scientific nomenclature of plants and anmals creating two latin names for every species. This system was adopted world wide, and still enables the communication between scientists, gardeners, birdwatchers, etc.

ABOUT MARIKA
Karen Messing

As a biologist I know little about history as an academic field, but it seems to me that it takes a lot of both generosity and humility to devote one's career to documenting what others have done. Carefully studying past and present lives and times must require not only patience but devotion. My contact with Marianne Ainley while she was at Concordia certainly confirmed this impression. Establishing an institute for feminist research at Concordia required her to sacrifice time, money and sometimes tranquillity of spirit but she did her part willingly, while complaining much less than I would have!

I was most closely involved with her professionally when she was producing Despite the Odds: Essays on Canadian Women and Science (Véhicule, 1998), a book devoted to celebrating Canadian women scientists. I remember the passion with which she urged us not to throw away our files (and our inability to understand why our old papers about long-disproven theories would interest anyone). We were all proud of the finished product. She assembled the cream of Montréal's women scientists for the launch and it was lovely to see my former professors delight in having their struggles recognized and celebrated.

Marika at the lectern

AN UPPITY WOMAN
Anne-Marie Weidler Kubanek

In the fall of 1977, I was hired as a part-time lecturer at Concordia University to teach introductory chemistry at the Loyola campus. I had done my education at Uppsala University, Sweden, studied a year in California, and worked in industrial research at a chemical firm in New Jersey before coming to Canada with my family. My first teaching position in my new country had been at John Abbott College. By the spring of 1977 there was no more work there for me so I felt myself lucky when I landed a job at Concordia. I was put in charge of the general chemistry labs and taught some evening courses in organic chemistry. That is when I met Marianne Ainley.

We did not see much of each other during that year at Concordia. Marianne was a research assistant and demonstrated some labs in the chemistry department. In the spring of 1978, neither Marianne nor I had our contracts renewed, as the newly-hired department head did not see the need for our services. It is in connection with that dismissal that I have my first vivid memory of Marianne.

One morning in May, I received a phone call from her. She wanted to know what I was planning to do about, as she saw it, the unfair treatment of the two of us. "What is there to do?" I probably answered, although I can't remember my exact words. However, I do remember my impatience with this woman who seemed to think that two lowly part-timers, women to boot, had any right to feel indignant over a summary dismissal.

At the time, I had spent my entire professional life, studying and working, in a male environment and was blind to any unfairness in the way women in science were treated. All my bosses and most of my colleagues had been men, and without much reflection I had cheerfully accepted the role as an anomaly rather than a respected colleague. While Marianne probably had hoped for some words of solidarity from another woman treated shoddily, I dismissed her concerns. As I hung up the phone after our brief conversation, the thought going through my head was, "This woman does not know her place." It is a testament to her generosity that we later became friends.

Fast forward to 1990! Since 1979 I had been back teaching chemistry at Montreal area CEGEPs, first at Vanier College and later at John Abbott. But more importantly for my professional as well as my personal life, over the years my eyes had opened up to a new reality. It had happened gradually through contacts with colleagues at the Women's Studies Program at my college and through events, some of which had shaken me deeply, above all the killings in 1989 of fourteen young women at Montreal's École Polytéchnique, including one of my former students from John Abbott.

As I walked the corridors of John Abbott College, what struck me now was not just the obvious fact that the vast majority of the science teachers were male, but rather that there was an almost total lack of recognition of women's contributions to science in textbooks, in audiovisual materials, or in the many pictures of accomplished scientists adorning the walls of my college. The thought that this milieu must have an effect on the many female science students had prompted me to start planning an educational research study with Margaret Waller, a sociologist and a strong feminist, about the experience of the young women in our science program.

Then one morning I saw a review in the *Montreal Gazette* of a new book, *Despite the Odds: Essays on Canadian Women and Science*, edited by Marianne Gosztonyi Ainley. I read with fascination about this accomplished woman who had arrived in Canada via Sweden, my own home country, after the Hungarian uprising in 1956. She had received an M. Sc. From Université de Montréal and a Ph.D in history and philosophy of science from McGill University, and was now teaching a course on "Women, Science, and Technology" at the Simone de Beauvoir Institute at Concordia University. As I was contemplating the possibility of auditing her course it suddenly struck me. I know this woman: she is the "uppity" technician from Loyola Chemistry Department. I was awestruck! What a courageous path she had chosen and how successfully she had transformed herself from lab technician to university professor. When I picked up the phone to call her to enquire whether I could audit her course, my tone of voice was, needless to say, quite different from our last conversation in 1978.

Marika welcomed me with open arms. My contact with the Simone de Beauvoir Institute and Marika became a lifeline and a refuge from my daily life with colleagues at John Abbott, who would think nothing of referring to all students as "he." I learned to appreciate the small cups of espresso coffee she served in her office. I was invited to take part in her panel discussions and to talk to her students about Ellen Gleditsch, a Norwegian woman scientist whose life I was studying and writing about.

I have never known a successful woman scientist as generous with her time and support of other women as Marika. She challenged me to take on projects. She assured me that I could write a compelling story if I put my mind to it. She complimented me on what I had done and pushed me to do more. And with Marika around there was fun and there was laughter. In 1999, as I was getting ready to retire, we spent a week together in a cabin on a campground outside Tromsø, Norway. Six of us, friends and students of Marika, and her husband David, were all crammed together in a very small space. We had met up in this town far north of the Arctic Circle for the conference "Women's Worlds 99, the 7th International Interdisciplinary Congress on Women." Despite many excellent presentations and an awe-inspiring mid-summer celebration under the midnight sun, the highlight of the week for Marika was her encounter with a rare upland sandpiper, fjällpiparen, in the mountains above Tromsø. Sometime later I received a drawing from her of this colourful bird with the city and the distant fjord in the background.

Marika, to say you were yourself "a rare bird" sounds disrespectful of a feminist scholar. But in my sadness of knowing you are not any longer stalking birds in British Columbia, watching out for bears which, as far as I know, were the only creatures on this earth that you were afraid of, I can find no better words to describe you.

Bird's Eye View of Tromsø. A female dotterel fjällpiparen. Painting by Marika, of Tromsø, Norway, 1999. Photo by David Ainley

MOTHERING THE MOTHERLESS - FEMINIST LESBIANS IN THE ACADEMY
Theresa Healy

I can't say Marika was my friend – not in the same privileged way some of us can. My relationship with Marika was different; it had an element almost of parenting. You see, the university is not an easy world to enter as a woman, even less so as a feminist and completely intimidating for a lesbian. But it was made easier for some of us by Marika. She was able to decode the most puzzling behaviors and policies and map a course of survival for the newborn academic. She was able to post some milestones and guideposts through the rocky and unfriendly landscape of the centre of male privilege and discourse.

When I arrived at UNBC, she showed up in my office with books she thought I should read. She gave me copies of articles that she thought would work for classes I was teaching. She gave me her personal copies of hard-to-get-hold-of lesbian novels when I started prepping for Gender Outlaws, a class focusing on the "lives of lesbian and bisexual women." This was one of the earliest classes of its kind in Canada when even mentioning the word lesbian in an academic context was thrilling and dangerous and before we embarked on post-modern fluid and shifting sexualities.

It was her open embrace of this more radical and challenging aspect of my university career that came to mean so much to me. I wasn't any less of an academic because I was gay; I warranted the same support, the same interest, the same challenge as any other feminist scholar. She took my enthusiasms with the same seriousness she gave to everyone else's pet projects. When my partner and I became part of the same sex marriage case, she told me how proud she was of me and what we were doing. She came to our wedding, once we had - unexpectedly and a lot faster than anticipated – won the case. She created a multi-media work to commemorate both the battle and the ceremony. That painting has a proud place in our home, since the day she gave it to us.

Marika was ahead of her time in some ways. Her comfort and ease with all the facets of who I am – feminist, newbie prof, lesbian, same-sex marriage advocate – was supportive of them all in unfailing good temper and a fine sense of humour. I am so sad that the newer generations of feminist scholars and artists will not have this priceless good-humoured mentor to ease their journey, that they will not have the pleasure of trying to keep pace with her energetic stride around campus and watch her eyes sparkle with delight as she skewered yet another too-easy target. She gave so generously and the legacy she leaves behind is a poor substitute for her presence. But, it is also more than enough to light our way.

Rose Breasted Grosbeak. Photo by E. Tina Crossfield. Ontario, 2014

MOVING THROUGH LIFE: REMEMBERING MARIANNE
E. Tina Crossfield

I once told her that she could fit into any generation, and communicate effectively with anyone regardless of age, gender, language, and the complexities that define our lives. Marianne was a force in motion, sometimes hard to catch, and forever looking ahead to the next challenge. Our last conversation was in May 2008, when I recommended her as an academic supervisor for a female colleague pursuing her master's degree, knowing that her expertise on women in science would be invaluable. Sadly she declined, saying that her health was the number one issue now. It was a project that she tackled with great energy and hope. She was my friend, my mentor, my advisor, at times more demanding than my mother, and one of the best scholars of her times.

I met Dr. Ainley after reading her book, *Despite the Odds*, which I found in a small bookstore in NDG. I was surprised to discover that she was teaching at Concordia University's Simone de Beauvoir Institute in Montreal, and I needed another course to compliment my term. The problem was that I could not attend her lectures until the third class that session. "No problem," she assured me, "here's the reading list." I came to believe that that's what Women's Studies is all about – giving someone an extra chance when the odds were not in his or her favour. Throughout my own career, I have tried to follow her example whenever possible.

We got along well from the start. She insisted that I call her Marianne because she insisted that most people could not pronounce Marika very easily. When I was an undergraduate, she hired me as a research assistant, and invited me to attend conferences where she was presenting her research. We shared many hotel rooms, meals, and long drives in the countryside, all dotted with her spontaneous sense of humour. Later, she gave me an opportunity to co-publish an article with her on women in chemistry, followed by invitations to contribute to scholarly books on women in science.

I remember well the trip we made to Prince Edward Island to attend the Learned Societies Conferences in 1992. I drove her car and was instructed not to go faster than 100 kilometers per hour because it made sighting birds out the window nearly impossible. We stopped in Nova Scotia at Joggin's Fossil Cliffs where we proceeded to hunt for ancient artifacts, her second major interest. It was raining most of the day, and we got soaked even with boots and rain slickers, but came away with more rocks than we could carry. New fossils were appearing there daily with the Fundy tides, so years ago, people were actually encouraged to scout and collect. The area is now an important World Heritage Site and like many other excavations, visitors are asked to leave items in place.

During the same trip, Marianne's interest in First Nations culture increased. We attended a Native ceremony to repatriate skeletal remains that had been eroded from a beach after a storm in 1959. These bones had been held in storage for analysis until being returned to the local Bands in 1992. The ceremony took place at sunset, high on a hill overlooking the sea, where we formed a large and diverse circle of humanity and danced to drum beats and songs. On my right hand was Marianne, naturally falling into the rhythmic steps, and on my left was a uniformed RCMP officer whose arm was so rigid that I felt I was dragging him behind me. It was all rather surreal. Having missed out on supper, mainly because we got lost getting there and the restaurants were closed, we dined in our hotel room on orange marmalade, rye crackers and single malt scotch.

Later in the week, the local Native community invited us, along with other scholars, to participate in a Sweat Lodge and lobster feast on the Reserve. However Marianne and I decided to walk on the beach instead of crawl into a dark, humid and fiery hot tent made of spruce bows and other bits of flotsam and jetsam. She told me that as a child in Hungary during WII, she was often ushered into bomb shelters to avoid the violence and never was able to overcome the feelings of claustrophobia and terror that resulted from this experience. That evening the reward for taking a stroll instead was the marvelous sight of cream-coloured gannets diving and feeding in the waves. The feast, as prepared in the traditional way, was a fine affair coupled with fascinating conversation and storytelling.

After I finished my bachelor's degree at Concordia University, I followed Marianne's research, which led into an interdisciplinary master's degree. As my academic lead, she directed my program, which was divided between three disciplines and two additional supervisors. While doing my own research, I attended the Learneds Conferences again, this time in Calgary in 1994. We again shared accommodation, and took side trips to historical sites. One memorable visit was to Head-Smashed-In Buffalo Jump near Fort Macleod. Here we marveled at the 5,500 year-old archeological digs and climbed the steep hill in back of the Interpretive Centre to look for hawks. I have often recalled that outing as a very special time. How many students can say that during their studies, their academic meetings with supervisors took place while they were otherwise engaged in a mutually fun outdoor activity?

When my thesis was ready for review, I traveled to Prince George, BC, and stayed with the Ainleys. I was given the royal tour of the city and treated like family. We went birding together, discussed many lively topics, and worked hard on the editorial changes to my final draft. She could be a tough critic, as she wanted and expected the best from her students. She told me that of all the study and research that she, herself, had done over the years, she considered herself to be a writer at heart.

Marianne performed many selfless acts, and during our close association of more than twenty years, she never forgot my birthday. Once she emptied her clothes closet and gave me all the things she wouldn't wear again. She had impeccable taste, but confessed that some items were just misguided choices. Similarly, as part of the community at the University of Northern British Columbia, she was a great supporter of the arts. One evening when I called, she had just returned from the symphony. When I asked her what she had heard, she simply said it was another modern horror.

She followed my subsequent career, no doubt with much curiosity and amusement. While doing my first master's, I wrote a history of the Canadian Institute of Mining, Metallurgy and Petroleum after she recommended me to the centennial committee. I remember the interview as I was sitting around a large oval table with about twelve senior men. When I mentioned that I wanted to be very inclusive in my work, they told me that there were no women of any consequence to write about in their organization. My short answer was "We will see about that" as I vowed to my mentor to change that particular view. With Marianne's help, I was able to find and write about a number of influential women who made strong contributions to the fields of geology and mining.

I then began to look for further work having moved from Montreal to Calgary. As I struggled to find writing and publishing contracts, I took on a part-time job driving a yellow school bus. I am sure that I kept Marianne entertained with my adventures, which included rambling through the Foothills south of Calgary with twenty-seven elementary students and forgetting to release the hand brake. I could almost hear her roar with laughter over my emails. Finally she said, "I'm not sure what you are going to do with all of this, but it is interesting." She suggested I contact one of her colleagues at the University of Calgary and apply to do my doctorate. However, some things are meant to be and others are not. The timing was not right for me as my father had just passed away, and I could feel her disappointment.

As time went along, our communications became more sporadic. She spent several months at a time in Australia, and moved to Victoria, BC. I found employment with a community museum and archive In Okotoks, AB, and resumed my interest in book publishing. Then gradually returned to one of my former interests, that of pre-hospital emergency medicine. She knew of my second master's degree, in disaster and emergency management at Royal Roads, and whole-heartedly applauded my efforts. As I was completing my second thesis, I could not help but reminisce about my first degree and the wonderful assistance and support she provided.

It is hard to put into words the effect that Marianne had on my life. She helped me to understand and to analyze why things happened in certain ways, and taught me to question the history behind them. I began my working life as a lowly female technician in a hospital laboratory, even though I wanted to study medicine. I didn't understand the factors that blocked much of my path, or that of many other women in science, and why I was always so restless. *Despite the Odds* opened the door for me, and Marianne walked me through it. After that, I could never look at things again in quite the same way. It was a great gift.

Recently, I have taken up my binoculars to look for songbirds, as there are many unusual species in my backyard this summer due to changing weather patterns. Most of what I learned about birds can be traced back to outings with Marianne. She used to say, "Wait until they move and then you can see them in the branches." I know how to look for movement now, not just for what sounds pretty or stands still, but what is active and vibrant.

Marika and Tina Crossfield at Joggins Fossil Cliffs in N.B., 1992

Tina and Marika at Head-Smashed In Buffalo Jump, A.B., 1994

THE SONG SPARROW
Mabel McIntosh and Bob Barnhurst

"Marika often said that one of her proudest achievements was the instigation of the early morning field trips to Westmount Summit where she could indulge herself in the study of warblers and share her appreciation of them with so many willing learners. After moving to B.C., she sorely missed the "fallouts" of migrant warblers, which we so take for granted here in the east. Fortunately, she and David were able to complete their once-in-a-lifetime cruise to Alaska before she became ill and entered the hospital for the last time. We are sure that she had her binoculars with her. Marika will be much missed."

Bird Protection Quebec, vol. 51, no. 3, 2008, p. 8

Marika and Mabel McIntosh, BPQ

AN HONOUR
Sima Aprahamian

I had the honour to have known Marianne Marika Gosztonyi Ainley through the Simone de Beauvoir Institute, Concordia University. She was introduced to me by, I believe, either my colleague Homa Hoodfar who had invited me to attend an event in 1993 at the Institute, or Arpi Hamalian, whom I met at that event too.

Marianne Ainley was the Principal of the Institute at the time. I soon became a member and Marianne being a generous and welcoming person, invited me to take part in the research seminars and other activities. She also invited me to submit an application to teach a Women's Studies course at the Institute. She was always encouraging new scholars such as myself to continue engaging in research and teaching. As the Principal of the Simone de Beauvoir Institute, Marianne brought into the Institute a lively group of Research Associates and Fellows and initiated the Biography and Auto-biography seminar series in parallel to the regular Research Seminars. It is there that I started to do research on the works and lives of women anthropologists. Sally Cole, a colleague and an active participant, then organized a full day panel at the Canadian Anthropology Society meeting at UBC in May 1994 on biography/auto-biography, held in the beautiful Museum of Anthropology. My presentation became part of the section on women's work in Canadian anthropology. Marianne recorded the entire whole day session. It is at UBC that I saw first-hand Marianne's love and passion for birds. She had her binoculars with her. We walked by the museum's nature path and admired the many different bird species she joyfully recognized. Soon after, in 1995, Marianne left Concordia University. Our friendship continued through e-mail and at meetings of the Canadian Women's Studies Association. I appreciated her care and support very much.

LUMINOUS ROLE MODEL
Rose Tekel

Let me begin by outlining my relationship with Marika, as I think it says a great deal about the spirit and power that Marika affected on many people throughout her life.

I did not know Marika while I was living in Montreal, as I moved away before Marika became involved with the Simone de Beauvoir Institute. However, the name Marianne Ainley (Marika) started to become part of my conversations with Susan Hoecker-Drysdale, as Susan and Marika developed a close working and personal relationship. During one of these conversations Susan mentioned to me that friends of Marika were looking for someone to translate an autobiography of a woman Polish scientist for a collection of essays they planned to publish. The friends in question were Marlene F. Rayner-Canham and Geoffrey W. Rayner-Canham and they wanted to publish a book which dealt with forgotten women in the early era of research on matter and radioactivity. In their preliminary research they had found an autobiography by Alicia Dorabialska, who had worked in the field of chemistry. It was, however, only available in Polish and had to be translated before it was clear if her contributions in the study of radioactivity could be discussed. One day Marika phoned my mother - Stephanie Weinsberg-Tekel - and asked if she would be interested in undertaking such a task.

My mother, who had spent much of her life doing translation from Polish to English and German, was delighted to take on this work. She discussed the details with the Rayner-Canhams and went to work on this new and very challenging assignment. She worked very diligently on the translation and subsequently it was decided that she would write a chapter entitled "Alicia Dorabialska: A Polish Chemist" in the collection of essays about women scientists called A Devotion to Their Science: Pioneer Women of Radioactivity.

My mother also had several telephone conversations with Marika and had wide-ranging discussions with her about women in science, as well as women in modern society. After each of these conversations, my mother returned to her task with renewed energy. Finally she finished her paper and sent it off to the editors. Eventually proofs arrived and we both further edited the paper. We now waited anxiously for news of the actual publication of the volume. The book was published in 1997, unfortunately after my mother's death.

We had met Marika and her husband David, as they had visited us in North Bay, Ontario, while en route to their new home in northern British Columbia. We discussed our experiences in Montreal as immigrants from Eastern Europe, and also talked about living in northern areas of Canada. We did not spend much time together; however, we very much enjoyed the experience. Several years later, I had another opportunity to enjoy Marika's company, this time at the Eastern Townships home of the Hoecker-Drysdales. Therefore, my relationship with Marika was basically one of acquaintance - someone I had only met twice. Yet this woman had a very profound impact on both my mother's life and my own.

Marika had linked my mother with the right people and the right project and gave her support while she was engaged in the project. My mother was already in her mid-eighties when she started this work. It gave her an enormous sense of accomplishment to be able to make a contribution to scholarship - especially in the field of Women's Studies - at that stage of her life. Because she was doing this work, she saw her identity as a writer and researcher rather than as a very elderly, housebound lady. She and I were now able to have discussions about issues in writing and research dealing with women's lives. She often would talk to other people about the work she was doing and explain why it is so important to document and discuss the contributions of women that have often been neglected in the past. It gave her particular satisfaction to have these conversations with many of her young friends. She was once again using the many skills that she had honed throughout her life: translator, teacher, and feminist.

I wanted to make this story public because of something Susan Hoecker-Drysdale had said to me shortly after the death of Marika. Susan told me that Marika had had such a great impact of the lives of so many people, young and old, and that we would never know these stories. Now we know at least one.

In the forward to the collection of essays Marika had written, the last paragraph appropriately summarizes the purpose of the book and I think the contributions that Marika has made to many people's lives. Marika wrote:

The feminist biographical approach of this book will lead to changes in the conventional story of radioactivity. By recovering forgotten women and presenting them as active, creative agents whose work had a major impact on the scientific discoveries of the last century, the authors give us a different, much more complete story that will help in reinterpreting the history of science.

The story of Marika, I would like to suggest, is the story of a woman who was an active and creative agent of connections among women and the knowledge that they could share and shape for future generations. And it did not matter if your connection with Marika was - as in my case - only brief, as it was nevertheless quite profound. Marika truly lived the life of a scientist, teacher, and feminist, and in the process provided the rest of us with a luminous role model.

MY YEARS WITH DR. MARIANNE AINLEY (1989 TO 1995)
Nilima Mandal Giri

In September 1989, I joined the Simone de Beauvoir Institute, Concordia University, as an Adjunct Fellow. I was provided with an office on the 4th floor of the Institute. One day I was working in my office with the door closed. Suddenly, there was a knock at the door. I responded and opened it. There was Marianne with her smiling face. She introduced herself saying, "I am Marianne Ainley. Arpi downstairs told me to help you in your research. Can I help you?" That sentence touched my heart because nobody in my life until then showed any interest to help me in my research which I was eager to do. From that moment we became good friends. When I joined the Institute, Marianne's position was an Adjunct Fellow and her office was next to my room. After a few years, Arpi left and Marianne was hired as the Principal of the Institute, and her office was on the 2nd floor. During the years while she was an Adjunct Fellow and the Principal, our friendship grew closer, and continued while she was in BC and it lasted until she passed away in September 2008. Many of our friends call her Marika. But I prefer to call her Marianne, as that is how she introduced herself to me.

Marianne was an intelligent, bright, kind-hearted, and helpful woman. In addition, she was a prolific researcher and writer. Since we met, she became my mentor and a good friend. I will provide a few examples which will indicate her role as my mentor and the nature of our friendship while we were at the Institute. She realized that to raise my status as a researcher a few things were essential, such as finding a research project which would be original and contemporary, publishing some papers, attending some conferences, and presenting research papers in the conferences, etc. She encouraged me for each and every one of these things.

She volunteered to come to my house within a few days of our meeting and went through all my past research work… We decided that an appropriate topic would be the professional immigrant women in Canada. So I started to read the literature on that subject. One day she telephoned me to come down to her office. I went down. She told me, "You have to apply for a research grant today." I was surprised because I had no idea of the topic I would work on until then. Marianne, as a researcher and writer on women in science, encouraged me to do research on South

Asian women in science. She told me, "You just hit me. I did not include a single South Asian woman in my writings." I hesitated and asked, "You are my friend. How can I hit you?" (Obviously this phrase was lost in translation.) She suggested that I go to my office and outline the project as soon as possible. I came down with a written project on "South Asian professional women in science in Montreal" within an hour. She edited it, and we mailed it the same day. Subsequently, I received a research grant from CRIAW. That was the first grant of my life, enabling me to do my research. I completed that project in two years. She was delighted at my success. She mentioned my work in several of her lectures and books.

She suggested that I write a few articles from my research work and publish them in the related journals, which I did. She encouraged me to present a few papers, not only in her 'Women in Science' class in the research seminar at the Institute, but also at the Learned Society's Conference, which was held in Montreal. I would not have had the confidence to present papers in public without her encouragement and help.

She advised me to attend conferences. I listened to her advice. Most of the time I paid for the travel and related expenses myself to attend the conferences. Once she decided that we would go together to a conference in Toronto. She arranged our first class fare on VIA Rail. I was delighted to be with her. Unfortunately we did not get rooms side by side in the hotel, so we stayed at night on different floors. She was so concerned for my safety that she could not sleep at night. The next day she came down in the early morning to my room to be sure that I was all right. After two days we left the hotel and started walking towards the train station. I was a slow walker, which was just the opposite of her. So she offered to carry my carry-on suitcase in addition to hers and asked me to "Walk quickly." I felt badly about slowing her down, but I was compelled to listen to her. Finally we arrived to Central Station and came back to Montreal. It was a memorable trip for me.

Marianne was a very broad-minded and caring person, which helped to strengthen our friendship in a short time. I had a very nice time at the Institute during the period she was the principal. Very often she phoned me at noon with an invitation to have lunch together in her office. We would talk about our family, health, food habits, etc. After lunch we used to go out for a short walk. I remember one day we suddenly saw a Sale sign in front of Ogilvy's department store. We went inside the store and noticed that some women's dresses were on sale at 75% discount. She was so excited and found a nice royal blue jacket and skirt in a small size. Then she advised me to buy it. At first I did not want to, because I had never worn a skirt in my life and it was an expensive outfit. Luckily she didn't like how the skirt fit on me, but she insisted I buy the jacket. Even though it was hard to find the money to pay for it, I was unable to argue with her, and she talked me into it. I followed whatever she said. She loved to see me wearing a Sari (Indian woman's dress). Whenever we had any social gathering at her, or any of our friend's houses, she always insisted that I put on a Sari, which would indicate my cultural identity. Now whenever I see that lovely blue jacket in my closet or I wear a nice Sari, I remember her.

Marianne used to come to the Institute in the early morning and park her car a few blocks away from the Institute towards Atwater. She gave me a ride back home many times. Sometimes I did not want to go with her because the parking spot was quite far for me to walk. She used to tell me, "What is wrong with walking? Walking is good exercise for your heart. Let's walk." So I had no choice but to walk, albeit reluctantly.

She widened my circle of friends introducing a birthday Lunch among her very close friends, such as Susan Hoecker Drysdale, Barbara Meadowcroft, and Katherine Waters. She included me in that group. They all became my good friends. They invited me many times to their houses. We still look forward to our birthday lunch. We always keep in touch and get together. In conclusion, Marianne helped me to feel a sense of belonging in academia and in the Concordia community. I never thought she would leave Montreal. In 1995, when she decided to go to Prince George, I felt a kind of vacancy in my life. Although she left Montreal, our friendship continued. We were always in touch either by email or telephone. Whenever she and David (her husband) visited Montreal, they came to my house. She gave me so much in my life – I am grateful to her.

I never thought she would die so soon. I wish her peace in Heaven. I will cherish her help and genuine friendship in my heart as long as I live.

COMPOSING A LIFE
Sally Cole

I first met Marika on my birthday, September 18, 1992, a few weeks after I had started a tenure-track appointment at Concordia University. I attended a reception she was hosting, as Principal of the Simone de Beauvoir Institute, to welcome faculty and students back to start a new academic year. A friend from Trent University, Chrystal Verduyn, who had also moved to Montreal that year to spend a sabbatical as a Visiting Fellow at the Institute, had invited me to come with her to the reception. I was looking forward to meeting other feminists. With her commanding presence, red hair and large dark-framed glasses, Marika sailed across the room to introduce herself and to tell me she had heard so much about me. She made me feel welcome and valued – an immeasurable gift to a new and junior scholar in the competitive and ego-riddled world of academia. Every year after that, she remembered my birthday with a card, or book, or phone call.

I had moved to Montreal from Peterborough, Ontario, with my two children, Sam, then-5 years old, and Bella who had just turned 3. My partner, economic historian, Michael Huberman, was tenured at Trent University; he remained in Peterborough during the week and commuted to Montreal on weekends until he obtained an academic position at the University of Montreal two years later.

Marika was so generous. I was new to the city and my kindred-spirit mothers-of-young-children friends were now geographically distant. Throughout that first year, she would phone me at least once a week with suggestions (directives) of things to do with the kids: "There's a puppet show this weekend at the Fraser-Hickson Library." "Take them to the Eastern Townships this weekend to see the huge flocks of migrating snow geese resting in the fields." "It's apple-picking time." "There's a pumpkin exhibition at the Botanical Garden." I'll never forget one cold afternoon in late November when I was working at my desk in the kitchen preparing classes for the next day. Marika called me to say that there was going to be a power failure and I should boil some eggs right away before I went to pick up the kids at daycare. I didn't know what she was talking about! She explained that that's what they did in Europe during the war: they'd hard-boil eggs so they'd have something to eat when the power went out.

It was such a relief to me to be able to talk to Marika: at that time she was the only person I knew in the city who acknowledged that I was both mother and scholar. Whether imagined or real, in my own Department I felt that I needed to present and maintain a single identity as a scholar and a career-minded academic. Under Marika's attentive eyes, by contrast, I always felt a responsibility to be a whole person.

She was instrumental in helping me to develop my personal "seasonal round." Not knowing that I would be offered a tenure-track job at Concordia (I was on my third post-doctoral fellowship at the time), Michael and I had bought a half-finished cottage on a small lake on the eastern side of Algonquin Park. It was one and a half hours from Peterborough where we then lived - but it was far from Montreal. We weren't sure what we were going to do with it now that we were working toward building a life for ourselves and our children in Montreal. When the first summer came – the summer of 1993 - I was feeling tremendous pressure to write and "produce." But I also wanted my kids to have time outdoors swimming and playing away from the city and away from the routines and structure of daycare life. Marika - who loved the Canadian wilderness more than many Canadian-born Canadians – loved the idea of the cottage and fondly remembered her own summers spent camping with her children when they were young. In authoritative tones and in so many words, Marika shared her life experience and gave advice to this mother-scholar: "Your son will only be five once. You only have one chance to spend this summer with him. Before you know it they'll be grown and gone. You can write then. Enjoy your time with them now. The academy will always be there." And so I snuck away from the university to spend a month with my kids at the cottage that summer – and every summer afterward until they were - as she said they'd be – fledged and making other plans for their summers. As I've said, Marika *expected* me to be a whole person – a friend, a mother, a scholar, a teacher, a good colleague, a caring citizen, a lover of nature. And because her values were also those by which I was trying to live and measure my own life, her expectations also gave me license to work toward integrating these values into my life each day. The details of Marika's life (which others in this volume describe) exemplify how hard she herself worked and how creatively she innovated "composed" (ref. Mary Catherine Bateson, *Composing a Life*) - her own life course. She freely passed on to others the joys and importance of authoring one's own life.

Our friendship matured as we shared our research as feminist scholars. In our scholarship, we both sought to make visible women's often unrecognized contributions to knowledge and to document the creative ways in which particular women had lived their lives and the diversity of models these lives offer to those of us seeking to live full lives as women in this world.

I was hired as an assistant professor in the Department of Sociology and Anthropology at Concordia. I came as an active field anthropologist whose research was in the area of gender, migration and development. After finishing my Ph.D. at the University of Toronto in 1987, I had spent several years as a migrant scholar living on postdoctoral fellowships and part-time teaching at several different universities. Tenure-track jobs in anthropology were scarce. Partly as a reflexive exercise on the difficulties I myself was experiencing in securing a permanent academic appointment, I had started to develop a second area of research: the history of women in anthropology. At the time, there was little research and publishing in this area in anthropology. Field-based research was – and is -- more highly regarded in the discipline. As an untenured scholar it was risky to be taking this direction in my "career." Marika, however, was fascinated with my idea to write a critical feminist history of anthropology through the life of one anthropologist, Ruth Landes.

Ruth Landes had been a contemporary of Margaret Mead and had been trained by the same teachers at Columbia University: Franz Boas and Ruth Benedict. Landes had written two of the earliest ethnographies devoted to women's lives in different cultural contexts: *The Ojibwa Woman* published in 1938 based on her research with Canadian Ojibwa and *The City of Women* published in 1947 and based on her research in Salvador, Brazil. Marika encouraged me to pursue this project and helped me to develop a professional context within which to locate this research. She integrated me into her network of feminist scholars who were working on the history of women in science. She invited me to join her on panels at feminist conferences. She initiated a Fellows Seminar on Biography and Autobiography at the Simone de Beauvoir Institute where I presented my research on Ruth Landes and met like-minded scholars in Montreal. And she was one of the biggest fans and promoters of the resulting book, *Ruth Landes: A Life in Anthropology*.

Marika provided, by example, so many lessons in living. There is one final one I want to write about here. As it happened, her mother, Sári, lived in the same apartment building in Montreal as my in-laws, Ruth and Leon Huberman, and directly across the hall from them. Sári died in 1993 and I went to the funeral at Paperman's Funeral Home. There, I was surprised when it was Marika who walked up to the microphone to give the eulogy. I remember thinking: "How can she get up in front of all these people and speak about her mother when she is suffering so much grief?" For, Marika dearly loved her mother. Dressed in an elegant black suit and a wide-brimmed black hat and her trademark big dark-framed glasses, Marika spoke eloquently and movingly about her mother's life during the war as she and her husband and two daughters had fled Hungary as refugees and lived in Sweden before emigrating to Canada. Two years later, remembering Marika, I did the same at the memorial celebration held when my father died unexpectedly at the age of 71. I had always felt very close to my father and I know now that speaking about him to those gathered to celebrate his life helped me both to mourn his loss and to keep him close to this day. It was Marika who, once again, had shown me the way. I am eternally grateful to her for this and so many other gifts.

KINDRED SPIRITS
Lynn Box

It was a fortuitous meeting of kindred spirits when I first met Marika Ainley. I had enrolled at UNBC the year before, but the actual campus and core programs were not introduced until 1992. Women's Studies was a cornerstone program that I was interested in, and I was fortunate to take my first course with Marika. This grassroots introduction to feminism changed the way I looked at the world and began a valuable friendship that was cut short far too early. Marika mentored me through my B.A. (1999) and encouraged me to pursue a M.A. in Gender Studies (2003). Her unwavering belief in my abilities and unconditional support of my thesis work made possible a dream that I never expected to achieve.

Marika expanded my horizons physically, emotionally, mentally, academically, and any other way in which one person is able to mentor another. While I was doing my M.A., Marika encouraged me to attend an international school in Latvia. This was the first travelling that I had done on my own and I learned I could, after that, manage anything. What a confidence booster. The trip to Latvia was the first of many that I undertook solo travelling, none of which would have happened if it had not been for that first (gentle) push from the Prince George nest. I met Marika and David in New Zealand in 2003, where she encouraged me to present a paper on my thesis to a history conference. This was a particularly memorable trip as we adventured to outlying islands to see bird habitat that I know I would not have experienced otherwise. She taught me a new way of seeing and provided me with an awareness of the natural world that I now carry with me, always.

Once my academic career was completed, Marika encouraged me to take up art and join artists' workshops. She was always experimenting and trying new mediums. Just when I thought I had a handle on one, she would introduce me to another. She provided the best art training: be prepared to take chances, look for happy accidents, and don't take yourself too seriously. I feel her with me every time I pick up a brush or pencil.

She was, and still is, the wind beneath my wings ... never to be forgotten.

Getting ready to head for home as the storm clouds build.
David, Marika, and Lynn Box, Tiri Tiri, Matangi, N.Z. 2003

Marika with Lynn Box at her graduation at UNBC, 2003

PROFESSOR EMERITA: THE STANDER
Jacqueline Baldwin

on the stage
Dr. Jacqueline Holler presents her
to the audience saying the name
Gosztonyi
with Hungarian emphasis
carefully cradling the word that speaks
Marika's family history

a melody of syllables and sounds fall into one another
the way a mountain stream makes music on
stones

she talks about Marika's worldwide reputation as a
renowned scholar of Science
reads a list of her publications,
appointments, accomplishments

the list is long

Marika Gosztonyi Ainley stands beside the podium
a woman with red hair in a red dress
before an audience of
seven hundred graduating students
more than a thousand parents, grandparents,
siblings, children, friends
fifty distinguished guests
one hundred members of the faculty and
a spectacular array of honorees and dignitaries

head high, she stands
composed, quiet
radiating certainty
listening
confident in the deep value of a life of dedicated work
calmly receptive to the honours bestowed upon her

although long gone from our gender studies classrooms
she continues to teach by example
this time, while accolades swirl around her
her lesson is about success

she is teaching us not to fear it
not to run away from it, nor
diminish its importance
but to stand proud and free
confident in the value of our own work
dignified in our pursuit of it

because she is Marika
the redness of her red dress
the serenity of her gaze
the way she holds her head

teach us
and because she is Marika
without saying a single word
all she has to do is

stand there

Marika presiding at the graduation, UNBC, 2003

THE HUNGARIAN FIRECRACKER
Annelie Dominik

Marika would tell people that I picked her up. Indeed, I picked her out of a room full of interesting people as someone I wanted to get to know better. So I introduced myself and asked her 'for a date'.

In Marika I found a kindred spirit with our shared interest in art forming the strongest bond. Marika approached painting with the same zest and vigor she applied to her life, loving the creative process in itself. Bold brushstrokes and vibrant colors infuse her paintings with energy and spontaneity. There was no 'pussyfooting around' in Marika's art making style. I think the term 'action painting' best describes her approach. I can see her now, spatula in hand, scraping away and re-applying paint to arrive at surfaces that are alive and have great emotional appeal.

Marika would return from trips all fired up and eager to translate her impressions into bold new canvases. She would often incorporate collected natural mementos into her paintings, which greatly enhance the tactile quality of her work. For example Techno-Totem has the sand of this Australian site mixed into the paint. This is one of David's favourite paintings. He says that it totally captures the spirit of the place.

One of the hallmarks of a good painting is that it challenges the viewer in some way. With Haida Gwai Totem, Marika set up very thought-provoking imagery when she juxtaposed a totem pole with modern day machinery.

Marika's paintings connect with the viewer through a theme, a message or an emotion in a very powerful way.

Like her personality, Marika's art making has many facets and she leaves behind a body of work that is astounding.

When I think about Marika now I do not envisage the academic, the scientist, the author or the painter, but a unique friend, the HUNGARIAN FIRECRACKER. Visualize it with me, the explosion of energy shooting up into the skies, transforming into an array of glittering stars and a rainbow of color, then descending and sprinkling us all with a little magic.

Thank you Marika for adding color and sparkle to our lives.

Annelie Dominik, Guestbook Art, 2008

BINOCULARS
Eric and Joan Jamieson

I think it was either the summer of 1996 or '97 that Joan and I were birding in the *Forests for the World Park* at Prince George. We were on the trail leading to Shane Lake where we stopped to look at a bird, when we saw Marika and David ambling along the trail. Marika, with her richly-coloured hair, scarlet glasses, jewelry, exotic accent and cosmopolitan air, seemed curiously out of place amongst the verdant slopes of a northern British Columbia mill town. But she had a set of binoculars slung around her neck and I've found that binoculars around the neck never lie. In fact, I've never met a birder I didn't like. We were soon to discover why she and David were there and further, that she was indeed in her element.

Joan and I were a little awed by this dynamic duo: Marika the academic and David the sports aficionado. I was a banker, perhaps not as staid as most in my profession, but a banker nevertheless, with all the sensibilities and cautions of one. It was Joan, the artist, who recognized another artist in Marika. They formed an instant bond, and despite their art styles being so diverse, it was the catalyst that cemented their friendship. Joan's colour sense was earthy, Marika's vibrant. But what brought the four of us together was the common language of the birder. "We saw a brown-headed cowbird near the airport," she said excitedly to us one Christmas bird count, "I could clearly see its yellow eye," as if this common bird should elicit the same sense of excitement that she reserved for the gift of the odd brambling or mockingbird that strayed into the north.

Marika was a skilled writer and author who punctuated her conversations with wonderful words that coming from anybody else would seem pretentious, but not so with Marika. Although she wore her academia on her sleeve on occasion, she was a strong advocate for learning. And the advice she gave me as a fellow writer and author was so relevant and timely that I will miss our many conversations about writing and publishing. In short, Joan and I are very sad to see the passing of this wonderful woman who was talented in so many ways. We will miss her dearly.

PROUD AND GENEROUS SPIRIT
Rae Marie Taylor

A year ago this past week, Marianne and I had e-mailed about the possibility of her and David's visit to Santa Fe, and the sorry timing that I would have to leave the old Spanish capitol before their hoped-for trip in May. That was a trip they weren't able to make.

How happy and energizing a time it would have been to be able to share my beloved Southwest with her. Fourteen years before, when New Mexico poverty had driven me back up to teaching in the north, Marika had been the first in Montreal to recognize my deep engagement in my writing and the importance of my homeland in that endeavor. She was the first to support early on the book I am just now finishing, recognizing its worth amidst the unruly material.

I remember our first contact. Hearing my discouragement that the Native American literature course I had initiated at Dawson risked dying along with my job there, a Mohawk friend, Audra Simpson suggested that the Simone de Beauvoir Institute at Concordia might be interested in First Nations Literature. I called, and easily reached the Principal, Marianne Ainley. Today the memory brings me not so much her voice, but her resonant presence still strong, keenly interested. Before we hung up she had invited me to join the Fellow Seminar on autobigraphical writing, and had restored my faith in possibilities for my work. Soon seeing her more in action, I learned to admire her as something of a powerhouse! Warmly human all the same, she was so amazingly quick to grasp the very real, just or unjust, dynamics of women's professional situations.

Marianne never ceased her support. She was always available to share her conviction that woman's work, women's creativity, my perspective as a woman, and my personal knowledge were so very valuable. She believed it so thoroughly that my own strength could only be revived and encouraged by hers.

I did teach a few courses in Native Literature at the Institute, which gave me a chance to see her and exchange with her on a collegial basis. Since she and David moved to Prince George, though, other than at a party or two during her visits to Montreal, I had not seen her in person.

But, we did stay in touch by e-mail. I keep the wonderful pictures of her paintings and herself, (one during her proud recovery from her first bout with cancer) that many of her friends must have too.

Marika's proud and generous spirit opened the door to a circle of admirably creative and professional women, equally strong and productive, teachers and writers "hors paire" and their own women: Dana Hearne, Susan Hoecker-Drysdale, Kathryn Waters, Barbara Meadowcroft.

It is still a bit hard for me to grasp that Marika, as she signed her e-mails, is gone. As I've continued with my work, I've been grateful for her unhesitating willingness to be among those all-important references for my application to Banff or submissions to journals. Some of her letters still sustain me in hard moments of doubt: "I love your writing," she might say "words so rare and sustaining to a poet!" as she put me in touch with other writers who would understand my concerns.

It is hard to feel I can properly witness the power of her encouragement, and the unique joy of sharing professional and creative concerns with her. I wish so much that I could call her this week and say "Marianne, dear friend, remember the book on the land I've been writing? It's done." Perhaps she can share my joy from somewhere in the cosmos.

Dorothy Appleton, Guestbook Art, 2008

Left to right: Susan Hoecker-Drysdale, Marika Ainley, Barbara Meadowcroft,
Dana Hearne, Katherine Waters. at Dana's home, Sept. 2007

Madronas Group: Annelie Dominik, Alice Webster, Bonny Myers, Shelley Wuitchik,
Dorothy Appleton. In front seated is Maureen Doyle; behind Marika and Dorothy is
Lois Badenhorst; Marika and Marsha Ross. Not present: Amy Nohales-Kezes, Janice
Graham, Marvin Arbour, Elizabeth Parnis, & Marilyn Robinson

LAST LETTER - SUSAN DRYSDALE
September 10, 2008

Dearest Marika,

I am sending this via Mark because the Post is so slow. There is a card in the mail but it might take a week or more to get there. At least "talking" to you in this way helps to maintain communication. It will be grand when we can talk on the telephone but right now you must rest and focus on comfort and recovery. The days seem empty without our conversations but I am thinking of you always and sending, just as all your many wonderful friends, waves of courage, strength and love.

It is definitely turning to autumn and even here in Washington the temperatures have dropped. The days are in the 70s (low 20s) now and the nights are cool. Occasionally we have a very warm, really hot, day but they are fewer and fewer. We have not had as much rain as we need here, so the view from my study displays some green, some yellowish, and some brown trees. The birds are active, planning their migratory trips, no doubt. And the hummers are busy at our feeder all day long. Unfortunately, so are the bees, who are utterly soaking up the nectar (sugar water). They all seem to manage. The mourning doves, sparrows, cardinals, bluejays, and nuthatches (white-breasted) gather happily on our two balconies in little groups, having cordial conversations. We do have gold finches in the neighborhood but they don't seem to come up this high.

You are having radiation treatments this week, which will probably not create major side effects and will fortify your system. And, if your experience is like your neighbour's (in the hospital), you will make some progress every day. Have you done any sketching yet? I heard that you asked for your pencils and book and makeup, all of which will help you feel happier. Did you enjoy the scotch as well? Maybe a nice glass of Pinot Noir or Sauvignon Blanc would be pleasant. I surely wish I were there to fetch it for you and to sit at your bedside while you rest. Hopefully soon we'll be able to talk on the phone, something great to look forward to.

I have contacted the acrylic painter, Dana Ellyn, (whose website you saw) who just came back from China and has a current show of her work there. Apparently, she is quite a political painter as well. She is having a party tomorrow night 6-8, so I'll go to see what she and her work are all about.

Well, Marika, I'll send this off to Mark so that he can bring it to you. I just felt I wanted to write to you privately. I have spoken with Barbara, Katherine, and Mary recently, and had emails from Sally and Dana. We're all rooting for you and send our thoughts and love. You are on my mind and in my heart every moment. Take care of yourself and think of our friendship.

John sends his love and warmest wishes for a smooth recovery as well.

Much love to my dear, dear Marika,

Susan

Robin Hood´s Bay

The Blog

Mark Ainley and Vicky Ainley

Marika's Process - September 4, 2008

We are starting this blog as a way for Marika's many friends to be in touch and updated as she goes through her healing process. Because of her vast social network, it will simply not be possible for her family to field all the caring phone calls and repeat the same updates; hopefully this blog can provide a way for her community to feel in the loop and updated.

The past week has been very tough as she has gone through a strong reaction to a new chemo, as well as to the pain-control medication. She is currently in hospital in isolation to build up her immune system, and is only taking family visitors. Though she is heavily medicated, she is still aware and able to communicate bits of information. She asked for a library book to be returned and her email checked, and to have her hair brushed.

Her main oncologist is excellent, as are the nurses at Emergency, so she is in good hands. David is of course very upset and concerned, and Mark is presently in Victoria as well, and Vicky will be arriving today.

We appreciate your thoughts and wishes. Feel free to share them here and we will communicate your hellos to Marika.

Evening update - September 4

The first post was written before we saw Marika on Thursday morning. She was still in Emergency - a really dark room in isolation, with no windows...not good for our outdoors-loving birder. (That said, the staff were amazing.) She was not very responsive this morning, being quite drugged out. The nurse did say that she had made excellent improvement on the thrush (not the bird variety) that had been plaguing her mouth and throat.

Vicky arrived midday and when we went to the hospital, Mum had been moved to the Cancer Hospice. She has her own room, and it has a window from which you can see trees and sky. She lit up when Vicky walked in, and was able to communicate despite her overall grogginess. She asked about world events and what was going on in our lives. "I'm in a right pickle," she stated - clearly her sense of humour is still working despite all the medication. Vicky virtually gave her a spa treatment, spraying her face with a water-spray bottle the nurses had given us, applying lotion to her back, hands, and feet...she could have been a Florence Nightingale if she hadn't gone into the wine business. It didn't take long for Mum to get quite tired, though, but she was fortunately more lucid than in the past couple of days.

When face-to-face with someone in this state, it is hard to imagine someone getting better, but this is apparently what the old days of chemo were like, and that's where this treatment took her. Unfortunately, the overall prognosis is still not good - the cancer has spread, though right now the main challenge seems to be the tough physical state she's in from the treatment one week ago.

Feel free to leave us messages on this page by clicking the 'comments' button below this posting, not the email button. Emails sent to Marika might occasionally be checked but this is the best way to reach us all. We very much appreciate your concern and best wishes.

One month ago...

This photo of Marika and David was taken on their Alaska cruise one month ago today. We are so glad that they were able to go on this trip and have such a great time. (see pg.31, in *Family*)

TGIF

We had a great visit with Mum this afternoon. She had been a little groggy in the morning again, but still affectionate and occasionally communicative. This afternoon she was livelier and more responsive - please keep in mind that this is all relative, in the context of being really quite drugged out and exhausted. But it was so lovely to see her smiling, and she was reaching for us lots, so we had some great hugs and kisses. Unfortunately kisses have to be behind the masks and gloves that we have to wear because she still has an MRSA (medication-resistant infection)

Her day nurse was wonderful today - very lively and caring. She encouraged us to continue doing up the room as much as we wanted - this after we took down the one tiny painting opposite Mum's bed and replaced it with one of Mum's own giant paintings. We also had a small CD player with mini-speakers in the background that were playing some classical music in the background (she requested some jazz for tomorrow).

We have been doing two visits a day because she has been so tired and even more so after our visits, but she was more energized today so we will have another visit after she rests while we have our dinner.

I have been sharing your messages and she appreciates them so much - please keep them coming, and thanks for being in touch.

Saturday Morning

We phoned the hospital to check in, and apparently Mum requested a strong, black coffee. Yesterday we had joked about bringing in a Scotch. (The nurse winked and told us to go ahead; unfortunately, Mum's mouth and throat haven't healed enough for that to be a good idea.) Yesterday she had a taste of some chocolate ice cream that she requested. Unfortunately she still isn't able to take much orally.

One espresso coming up, though...

What an improvement!

Your stated wishes, and ours, have been coming true. Mum showed huge signs of improvement when we saw her today. First off, she was wearing her glasses, despite being on her side in bed. She had her voice almost fully back, so she wasn't just whispering - what a relief to be able to communicate more clearly and to hear her character coming through more strongly!

And she certainly did come through loud and clear. She had a few words about her evening nurse ("Why do they always come disturb you just after you've fallen asleep?") [though all the other nurses we've met have been great] and had us draw up a huge list of things to bring in (including make-up and her sketch-book) and errands to run. The coffee no doubt perked her up (we gave it to her on ice), and she had a few more requests for edible items. Her digestive tract is still messed up inside, but her mouth is healing very well and so we hope she'll be able to start taking more food and drink before long. She's still wants the Scotch she asked for yesterday, but since it is quite harsh we may just give her a homeopathic dose diluted in water.

She was happy to see pictures of the art exhibit that she has some paintings in, and to get some cards. Please feel free to send cards and we'll take them in. We're going to do up the room while she's there - we asked about hammering in a few nails and putting more pictures on the walls. The cards will make a lovely addition too. She was also delighted to read the comments you wrote (and she was able to read them, rather than having me read them to her)

We're on a lunch break before going back for another visit. Will update again later. Marilyn's soup and Mario's gelato are on her menu for this afternoon...

Slower Sunday

Mum was a bit slower today - her throat was hurting her a bit more. We're not sure if it was the Scotch, coffee, or conversation that did it. She was still perking up at times, and Vicky once again put some make-up on her. She was excited to hear we had been to the exhibit yesterday, and that we had dropped off another painting for another exhibit.

She has made a couple of phone calls from her cell phone there, mostly to her sister and some overseas relatives. We also called the birdline and she was tempted to report that there was a baked turkey at the hospital. Her sense of humour is very keen these days, and she is appreciating everyone's comments and thoughts - we are sharing them each visit.

On lunch break now and returning shortly...

Sunday Evening

Mum's throat continued to hurt today. This afternoon we had a lovely visit in shifts, though. She got the television in her room activated, now that she has enough energy and waking hours to pay attention to it, so we made a date to go back to watch one of her favourite programs together at 9:00 p.m., a British police show called New Tricks.

She was not fully able to stay awake throughout the program, but enjoyed having it on in the background and we taped it at home for future reference. Unfortunately her throat is still giving her big problems - it seems that the skin inside is regenerating and so there is a lot of irritation. She has been given more medicine to help accelerate the process while also soothing the area.

This afternoon, just before I went in, the lady in the next room called me in and asked about what treatment Mum had had. She said that she recognized the kind of cough as what she herself had gone through after some chemo and stated that the 10-day mark where Mum is made sense - and this lady was sounding much stronger and clearer. "Everything that you're hearing is from the chemo," she said, "and she'll get through that." It was very encouraging. She also piped up in support when the nurse was at the door sarcastically announcing the arrival of more Jello, which Mum hasn't wanted to eat. "It goes down easy on the throat," called out the neighbour. Nice to know she has someone next door looking out for her!!

Mum still loves all your comments and is buoyed by your thoughts and wishes, as are we all.

Monday September 8

It was a busy day today - lots of visiting on different shifts as Marika's sister Gyongyi (say that ten times fast) arrived from Montreal. Mum continued to have a bad throat and is having trouble keeping things down. The very kind lady next door continued her words of support, stating that she was the same way a week ago and giving advice how to swallow Jello more painlessly (if such a thing could be possible - they do overdo it in hospitals, no?).

Gyongyi has years of experience in hospitals and set about getting the room wonderfully organized and cleaned. She was showering totally loving care on her sister and it was much appreciated. Lots of Hungarian flowing in the room, too, a nice nostalgic sound for Vicky and me (and maybe for Dad, though the verdict is still out on that one). Mum got more of the spa treatment - nails, eyelashes, and eyebrows. Lips, alas, have to wait until some of the swelling from the treatment goes down.

Mum will be starting a five-treatment series of radiation on Tuesday morning. This will be to focus on lessening the effects of the cells in the cerebro-spinal fluid, hopefully preventing them from latching on to parts of the brain and inhibiting whatever related functions are associated with that area. Fortunately the side effects from the radiation are far more minimal than those from the chemo - the nausea should be well controlled by some medication they will give her, and the tiredness that often goes with this is already present and will likely not be exacerbated. We're all hoping Mum will be back to her lively self once this throat challenge is overcome.

Good news is that her white blood cell count is much higher and that is helping her to heal more quickly. The MRSA is still present but we are waiting for tests that could mean that visitors don't need to wear masks - they will still need to suit up in the super-stylish yellow disposable gowns that we've been sporting.

Mum continues to be thrilled by your comments, and her room is starting to fill up with drawings from kids and cards from friends.

Tuesday September 9

Mum's voice is doing much better today - there was the strength that we had heard earlier in the week before the soreness came back with a vengeance. She has a new slurpy toy, the kind of suction thing that dentists use to pull out your saliva, so that is helping her remove some of the buildup without taxing her throat so much. As a result, she is speaking more clearly - and putting her voice to good use, as Dad wryly noted. Gyongyi is still there and taking wonderful care of her, and her cousin Robi will be visiting from Toronto on Wednesday.

She did have her first radiation treatment this morning - the doctors are quite certain this will help improve her quality of life by holding back the impact of the malignancy in her spinal fluid. No side effects yet, and they are certainly not expected to be anywhere as strong as those of the chemo she underwent over 10 days ago that she is still recovering from.

It is challenging for Vicky and me to be so far away for a couple of days - we had always stated that Victoria was close enough but far enough, but at the moment it's too far. We are looking forward to being able to visit on Thursday. We did read her the newer blog comments over the phone since Dad's technophobia might supersede that of some of the supposedly technologically challenged folks on this site, and she was very happy to hear them.

Movin' on up

Mum got moved into a room upstairs in the hospital today - don't have all the details yet but apparently the room is not yet done up to her specifications...her Feng Shui Consultant son needs to get in and work his magic, which will happen on Thursday.

Her voice was stronger again today and her cousin Robi arrived from Toronto - so there were three Hungarians in the room! If anything would get her voice working again, it would be that!

There was good news that the chemo session, for all the harm that it did, actually might have improved some of the liver functions for now, according to recent blood tests. That said, she will not have another such treatment as it would quite literally kill her - this last time was close enough (her reaction really was very, very bad). She had her second radiation treatment today to help hold back the impact of the cancerous cerebro-spinal fluid - three more of those to go.

A friend of mine was saying today that her mother had the same thing in her spinal fluid and that it didn't impact her the way the doctors had expected. It is always difficult to know how much of a doctor's expert opinion to take seriously because each person and their healing process is so different, so their diagnosis can often be nothing more than an educated guess - and guesses can be wrong. Here is hoping that she continues to defy the odds.

Thursday September 11

Vicky and I arrived today shortly after Robi left. Mum is able to sit upright and was looking very 'with it.' She'd done her eyebrows and put on her lipstick, and Gyongyi cut her hair, so she was definitely styling.

Unfortunately she isn't able to get much food down. She did manage to finish a whole serving of Jello with some ice cream, which is a big step, but she needs much more nutrition to get her body's strength up and to help her heal from the chemo. The sores in her mouth are still quite intense - I was really surprised to see how much is still there and can't imagine how much pain she must have been in earlier if that is what is still there. She's a tough cookie!

The new room will require some shifts in artwork to get the energy flowing better - I refuse to let Feng Shui considerations be overlooked! There is a huge TV opposite her that she was not thrilled about, although with an attached DVD player she now has the chance to watch some movies. That area is surrounded by many cards and photos that have been sent by friends and relatives. We will go through her artwork tonight and take some more when we have an evening visit after dinner.

A half-dozen cards arrived in the mail today, so she will be thrilled to have those too (we will take them to her so that she can enjoy them when she has more focus and energy).

We're hoping she continues to gain her strength and ability to eat - there is certainly no lack of desire on her part! As long as her body can cooperate...

Culinary Conundrum

We paid an evening visit to Mum and she had only been able to eat a bit. No wonder - the food they are bringing her is absolute rubbish. There was a strawberry mousse and a tomato-cream soup. Considering she isn't great with lactose and she has heaps of sores in her mouth, I don't know how they are thinking she will be able to eat this. And the answer is - they aren't thinking. The system is in place and unless conscious attention is drawn to it, diet is not considered.

We spoke with the staff and they were 100% in agreement that what she was brought was inconsistent with what she needs and they made a note to have a dietician visit on Friday so we can work at getting her things she can absorb that will be helpful. The staff is absolutely amazing - when they say they will check back in ten minutes, they are back in ten minutes; they are very considerate and helpful. There are angels working in this field, for sure.

But this demonstrates the fact that the squeaky wheel gets the grease. What about those who don't have family members or friends to complain on their behalf, or those who don't think to question things that the establishment should be aware of? The disconnect within the system is sad to witness and experience, especially when lives are at stake.

I've brought Mum some Aloe Juice with various supplements to help heal her internally and it was going down with ease. I'll be on the lookout for some healthy high-protein supplements in the hopes of getting her better nourished.

Toast to Marika

Some great pictures of Mum's friends toasting her at a recent art event.
http://marikaainley.blogspot.ca/2008/09/toast-to-marika.html

And Mum's two-part painting at that event

TGIF 2

Lots of time spent with Mum today. Vicky stayed overnight and both slept well, and Mum was awake and energized quite early on. She was going to be taken to have not only her radiation but also to have an ultrasound to make sure she was able to have a feeding tube put in, so Dad and I delayed our arrival.

She was in good spirits when she was wheeled back into her room - they have some interesting contraption set up from the ceiling that she holds onto to get into bed. Looks like a trapeze kind of thing, so we wonder if she'll be applying to Cirque du Soleil.

The throat is still really bad and she didn't get much more down today

- it is incredible to think that she hasn't had anything substantial to eat for probably ten days now. Unfortunately, the procedure to install the tube had to be postponed until Saturday because the Emergency Room got backed up with some pretty serious stuff.

It is also unfortunate that more of her hair is starting to fall out - and just after Gyongyi had done such a great job of styling it. She is still looking great, though - not that much has comes out - and she has a wig prepared if more comes out. But since there is only one more radiation treatment to go, she might still not lose it all.

Mum was delighted to see pictures of her friends at art events and giving toasts, and the guest book from the last exhibition was photocopied and hand delivered today, so she got to feel a bit more participative.

One of her doctors is a lovely aging gentleman who said to Dad yesterday, 'Where are you from, young man?" (They're about the same age). Turns out the doc is from Hebden Bridge, not far from where Dad grew up and where his cousin's daughter lives! Today when the doctor visited he stuck around for about 20 minutes and the two of them were swapping stories and dropping place names - definitely perked Dad up, and all of us, in fact. The staff has really been extraordinarily attentive and kind, but to find someone cut from the same cloth as Dad was an extra treat.

I will really have to start writing down some of the hilarious lines Mum is coming out with, because some of them really have been classics. Her sense of humour is there and comes out sometimes when we least expect it.

We brought in some more artwork and by Saturday she should hopefully have the pieces she wants in Feng Shui-friendly placement. Vicky will have to oversee that as I've had to come back to Vancouver because of some work commitments.

Gyongyi has been so touched and appreciative of the strong friendships Mum has been able to count on. "We should all be so lucky to have such great friends!" The cards, the calls, and the consideration shown by so many really has been extraordinary... thank you all for being there for her and for all of us.

Saturday Post

It's challenging for me (Mark) to be away on the weekend but with lots of work it was unavoidable.

Mum had the feeding tube put in. Unfortunately the hospital's schedule continues to be approximate at best. They told the family she was about to go in for the proedure, so we all left, and then they were delayed again so she was alone in her room for a bit before we figured it out and went to visit again until she actually did go in. The procedure went well and the tube appears to be pretty unobtrusive. The earliest they can feed her is 24 hours after the tube was put in, so you can bet that we will be watching the clock and making sure that she gets some nourishment as soon as possible! Here's hoping they have liquid Yorkshire Pudding and Wiener Schnitzel, and no Jello!

Mum's voice was sounding stronger and she was even more lucid - amazing considering the medication they are giving her, her state of hunger, and her overall condition. She is making really interesting observations and her sense of humour is more paprika-like than ever. Could it be the morphine? Whatever the reason, we're enjoying it!

The weather continues to be exceptionally clear and sunny, which certainly helps keep one's mood up - the sunlight comes through one of Mum's paintings, *Robin Hood's Bay in North Yorkshire,* which has been placed in one of the window frames, and it just creates a glow in the room.

Gyongyi was flying out early Sunday so had her last visit on Saturday evening after a dinner with the family and a close friend. Vicky was sleeping over in the room on Saturday and will pass along updates later.

Sunday Recap

A quick summary of Sunday - Mum started getting some food via her tube (no word on whether it was mashed Yorkshire Pud or Wiener Schnitzel) and was drinking some of the Aloe Juice that I brought her. She was sounding strong and clear already before this. This lack of food has been a good detox, and if anything has come out of it, it's very clear, soft skin!

More paintings have arrived to decorate the last remaining wall, and the cards continue to arrive and are all being put on the walls.

Sunday night was a family get-together watching *New Tricks* - the room has a much larger TV than that swing-around hospital one from last week.

More news to follow...

Monday Report

Mum didn't sleep that well last night - her IV machine (did Romans call them Four Machines?) was beeping and the staff didn't respond super-quickly to it. She was also a little tired from her radiation treatment today. Some good news is that her hair has stopped falling out, not because there is no more to fall out - presumably the ill effects of the previous chemo have slowed down now.

Mum's tastebuds were tickled with the delight of being able to not only to taste but *swallow* today! She's still just having a little bit, but she loved the ice cream and coffee (on ice) that she had today. She tasted a bit of tofu but needed a bit of coffee mixed with it to give it some flavour. There is still some residual blistering on her tongue but her lips are much better and she is so happy at being able to swallow. She is also getting food through her tube so she is definitely more nourished.

She continues to be happy at the paintings in her space, including a watercolour given by Dorothy, and also the funny books that have been gifted by friends. Cards continue to arrive too, and blog comments printed or read over the phone.

Photos of the room to come soon!

A Room With a View

http://marikaainley.blogspot.ca/2008/09/room-with-view.html

Tuesday Update

Mum had a very restful day - she had had a rather restless night. For some reason she hasn't been given a sleeping aid the past couple of nights. We didn't think that it would need to be requested but apparently so. As a result of this, and possibly also the tiredness that was said to be a side effect of the radiation, she spent a lot of the day sleeping. There is of course concern that it is her health that is shifting, but it seems likely that with her medication, radiation, lack of sleep, and adjusting to getting food, her body needs a good rest.

She had a few surprise visitors over the past few days, which thrilled her no end, but it seems that she does not have the energy she thinks she does and she tires very quickly. It is really difficult to find a balance between having the stimulation that her mind desires and the rest that her body needs. As much as she enjoys seeing everyone, we are not encouraging visiting at the moment while she recovers some more strength and so we can see just what factors are impacting her energy levels. More visits from out-of-town have been planned and that might be all she can handle at the moment, as much as we'd all like it to be otherwise.

You can see photos below of the room - the area with the cards around the TV is directly opposite her bed (and her Feng Shui consultant son would like the area tidied up a bit!). The lit painting is in the window opposite the door, to the right of Mum's bed, and the three paintings are on the wall to the left of Mum's bed, immediately as one enters the room. They definitely give the room a personal touch!

Wednesday Wake-up

Mum made an early-morning phone call with some requests, so she's back in action! She was sounding chipper and with-it, so clearly the rest was something she needed. We are going to encourage her to continue to take the time she needs so that she can have the quality of awareness and energy she seems to be enjoying so far today. She was so enthusiastic to hear that I would be there in a few hours and I'm looking forward to seeing her.

Wednesday

It was great to see Mum today - definitely a way better day than yesterday, much to everyone's relief. She continues to be very affectionate, and chatty about a number of things - art, friends and family, various things. Her energy levels do vary, though, and she needs to close her eyes and rest quite frequently. She is always concerned about those who are with her, shooing us out of the room while she rests lest we be bored - when I said we're not bored, she said "Quality, not quantity," and shut her eyes to rest.

There is, in some ways, much more quality too - her throat is infinitely better and swallowing is no problem, which enables her to get her medicine down, as well as occasional chunks of ice cream and healthier drinks that I've provided. Vicky and I have some reservations about what they are continuing to pass off in the name of food and will be raising those concerns tomorrow. (Vicky is here until the weekend, keeping up the manicures and pedicures, and more!).

Mum did some physio today - she sat up and did some resistance exercises to get some muscle tone back. (Her muscles have for obvious reasons very much atrophied). She was quite gung-ho and wanted to do some more but the physiotherapists wanted to make sure not to tire her out too much.

I brought Mum a stuffed Orca doll from BC Ferries - incredibly soft, much more so than the pillowcases at the hospital (not exactly 350 threadcount). She was happy to have a companion for the little platypus doll who also shares space in her bed when he doesn't get mysteriously relocated (he was hiding under the bed today). The nurses have commented that they never know what they'll find in her bed - a cell phone, platypus, make-up mirror...

The cards continue to arrive in hordes and we're almost running out of room on the wall opposite her bed (as seen in the picture in an earlier post) so we'll have to start decorating other walls too, it seems. She is enjoying those and her paintings. She asked if I could bring her some rocks, noting that there must be some in the car. I told her there would definitely be some in the car, along with sand, sticks, mud-caked boots, crumpled tissue, half-packets of Halls, and squished boxes of Band-aids. She laughed louder than she's been able to in ages.

I'll be flying back to Vancouver Thursday morning but will drop by to visit before leaving town - she seems to be in good shape in the mornings.

Thursday in a Nutshell

Quick update on yesterday - I had a quick visit with Mum before heading back to Vancouver and she was quite tired. She wasn't as chatty but of course still affectionate.

She got some great energy healing from Marilyn, and really slept most of the day. She is still giving her orders but a bit less verbally. Vicky and Dad of course spent lots of time with her - Vicky is still great at giving her the spa treatments!

She had some pain on her left side, and we suspect it might be the feeding tube - that is being looked into today.

Rest, rest, rest...it's what she needs at the moment.

Friday/Saturday

Friday and Saturday were quiet days for Mum. She was not speaking much - not really able to focus enough on it at times, which raised some concerns. A nurse finally pointed out today that a switch in pain medication might make her a bit more alert, and reviewed the case with a doctor and got the switch approved. This, of course, raises the question as to why it took so many days for this to cross someone's mind (and it's certainly not the first shortcoming in the very well-intentioned care that we've recognized). By Sunday we should know if there has been improvement.

While Mum has been resting a lot and fairly quiet when awake, she is good at using her arms to point out what she wants and needs when lacking the strength to speak. Her long-time friend and colleague Barbara is visiting from Montreal, and has been regaling Mum with stories so that she could lieback and get caught up on things without having to participate as actively.

Fingers are crossed that Mum will be able to be more awake and talkative, as we all know her and expect her to be.

Sunday September 21

Unfortunately, Mum's condition did not shift with the change in medication. She continues to be sleeping much of the time, occasionally waking but not for long. She is still doing her best, but the current scenario indicates what the doctors said would be happening as her body started to shut down. We are sorry to report that things are not looking good at the moment.

Mark will be heading to Victoria on Monday, and Vicky on Tuesday; Mark is scheduled to be in Vancouver to have dental surgery and teach on Wednesday, but that may change.

We are naturally very upset that Mum's continued valiant fight is not making the progress we had hoped to give her more time.

Please feel free to send comments to the family here; we will aim to verbally deliver messages to Marika, as we know she can hear us. We will read out bits of messages as we can.

And we will continue to keep you updated, and thank you for your thoughts and wishes.

Monday Afternoon

It is incredible how quickly things change. I was last here on Thursday morning; Mum was quite chatty Wednesday, and getting more tired on Thursday. Today, a mere 4 days later, she is really a shadow of herself. She is looking gaunt and is simply resting. She occasionally stirs, and she did open her eyes, but it is unclear how much she was aware of where she was or what is going on. We had been told that she would simply get more tired and sleep more and more, and that this is a peaceful way to go - we didn't think it would happen this quickly and suddenly, though.

I had a chance to speak with her alone, knowing that she can hear even if there are no external signs of that. My friend Naomi had given me three gemstones to give Mum, related to Love, Emotions, and Communication. Mum had the velvet bag in her hand as I spoke with her. It's now on her pillow, her stuffed platypus and orca lying beside her body as she rests.

I've been told by people who have been through the same thing to remember her as she was and not as she is, and I certainly do have in mind more how I knew her and not this frail body - Marika was always more than who she was physically. It is difficult, however, not to see that vibrant lifeforce radiating as strongly.

The doctors here are really wonderful. That British fella from Hebden Bridge is in this week and was spending some time chatting with Dad, and I really have not seen Dad that lively at all in some time. It is very helpful to have someone here who raises his spirits, as he is certainly having a very challenging time.

Thank you all for your lovely messages - they are so very much appreciated.

Tuesday Midday

Mum was much more responsive this morning - she was opening her eyes and we got glimmers of recognition. She is showing some moments of strength in her weakness, with a tight grip of the hand or the occasional attempt to sit up. When her friend Joanne from Prince George showed up, however, her face lit up and she smiled - very happy to see a friendly face from a while back! This was the first glimpse of her personality that had shown up for a while. Another came when she was lying with one finger above her lip: I said, "You're looking pensive", and she did a hand-swat while raising her eyebrows. There is more of her present than we can realize, and we are making an effort to continue to speak as if she hears everything, because we think she does.

Some of the synchronicity has been incredible. A lovely fellow emailed Mum just yesterday to say he had an ashtray that had been made by William Rowan (whose biography Mum wrote) that he wanted to give to her. We had a quick email exchange and he dropped it off at the hospice for us today - he was of course upset that she is as poorly as she is, but happy to have made the connection with us. Apparently he had taken over Rowan's office and he had left him his ashtray and pipe - and now they are in Mum's room! Thanks, George!

Vicky will be here this afternoon; Mark is still undecided about heading back to Vancouver for his dental surgery Wednesday morning to fix a tooth that started disintegrating a couple of weeks ago (it all happens at once, doesn't it).

Tuesday Night

Mum continued to be more active today than yesterday. She would wake more and clear her throat. She actually managed to turn herself onto her side when we weren't in the room - she's got more strength than she shows. "She's still keeping us on our toes and still running the show," the cheery nurse said. (The staff truly is exceptional.) Vicky arrived and the pampering continued.

And another Rowan connection today - the wife of Rowan's son Julian came in the same day Mum had been gifted with a hand-carved ashtray made by Rowan?!? What kind of incredible timing is this? Mum's face lit up again, much as it had when she saw Joanne's face this morning. It seems that older memories are triggering a very strong response from her; I mumbled something in Hungarian (which I cannot speak, other than a few words) and she responded quickly.

Mum is so tough that she continues to fight, and it is challenging to see her in this state. She is not comfortable per se, but clearly as comfortable as circumstances can allow. I am grateful that my memories of her are so powerful that these will supersede her last days.

I had a lucid dream experience with Mum in the early hours of Tuesday - I awoke in their apartment (but in the dream, as real as it felt) to find her, Dad, and Vicky all there. She was in good health, looking around, and energized. It was wonderful to sense her presence so fully. I had told her the previous day that she could always find a way to communicate with me, and I think she did.

The nurse called at 10:00 p.m. Tuesday night at our request, and said Mum was resting well. The doctor said patients are checked regularly, and when no family is present the nurses often sit with them for periods of time. She is being well looked after.

Wednesday

Mum had a mostly sleepy day today - some activity like yesterday, but not as much. She still has strength in her and is at times able to move herself, but she is mostly quite still. The degree of change since last week is just unbelievable. One nurse said some people can go through these extremes in one day, but it is still such a shift.

Julian Rowan visited today with his wife and had a few moments with her, but she was less responsive than yesterday. He was so pleased about the gift of the ashtray that had suddenly shown up, and of course so sorry to see Mum in this state.

Plans are underway to dedicate the upcoming Studio Madrona exhibit at Goward House to Mum. As Marsha wrote, "Hopefully this positive emphasis will resonate with her. Maureen and Alice (curators of this show) are planning to hang all of your mother's pieces together. As you know, her work is powerful, not only in content and message, but also in style. When shown together, the spirit of her works will fill that space of Goward House." This means a lot to all of us, as Mum's art was really such an important part of how she has expressed herself in recent years, and her friendship with the group at Goward House has been a key element in her life in Victoria.

Among the few words Mum stated when she was in rough shape a few days after the chemo treatment was "Celebration of life...Goward House...", and she made it clear that she wanted not a traditional memorial service but a celebration of her life to be held at Goward House. Her friend Gerry Dirks had been celebrated in a similar way after his recent passing, and she was clear this was how she wanted to be remembered - you know Mum, she loves celebrations and parties and a positive focus! Until the family arranges that celebration - she hasn't passed yet, after all - the art exhibition starting soon will be a wonderful way to honour her. Details of the exhibition will be posted here shortly.

Thursday

Mum was asleep the whole day today - her eyes did not open. She is looking very restful. Her heart is working overtime as various body functions shut down, but the result is that her cheeks have a warm glow, and she was looking very peaceful in bed. She was more unsettled a few days ago, as she waking frequently and occasionally calling out, as well as coughing.

We followed the suggestions of a number of people who have worked in palliative care by speaking with Mum individually to give her our blessings to move on; often people in this process can hold on for their family's sake. We first read some farewell messages that had been privately emailed and posted on the blog, and then each had some moments with her.

A nurse told us that with her current breathing pattern and other conditions, we were likely looking at 24 to 48 hours.

We apologize that we will not be able to call all of her many friends to personally inform them when she has passed, and know that it will doubtless be upsetting to read of it online. We know that it is coming, and simply wish for her to have a peaceful transition - it will be harder for those of us left behind.

At dinner tonight we talked about how quickly the change took place. Mark was visiting 4 weeks ago tonight, the day that Mum had the chemo treatment that would send her to hospital a few days later. That she managed to bounce back from that to be able to speak and spend quality time with us was a blessing, just as it was a blessing to have her in our lives to begin with. The kind words and support of her friends and family around the world throughout this process is evidence of how much she means to all of us, and we are grateful to all of you. Mum herself acknowledged how in this process she came to realize how much love she had around her.

Marika Veronika Gosztonyi Ainley
December 4, 1937 - September 26, 2008

Marika peacefully took her last breath at 5:34 p.m., surrounded by loved ones: her husband David, daughter Vicky, and son Mark, with her sister Gyongyi on a phone that was lying on her chest.

We are only taking phone calls from family at this time.

More to be posted in the coming days. Thank you for your love, support, and contributions.

Friday Review

For those who would like to know more about Marika's quite beautiful passing over, please read. If you feel that it will be upsetting to you, wait for the next posting that will cover more practical things. We are starting to surface and will slowly be taking phone calls, though it may take us time to return messages.

On Friday, Marika's breathing was quite pronounced - one might say she was snoring. She was completely unconscious, eyes not opening at all. Her breathing was quite rapid, and our dear Doctor Wilde from Hebden Bridge came in and said that she was very peaceful and that with these changes she couldn't continue much longer. This true gentleman's serene and compassionate bedside manner made it easier for us to take the news.

At about a quarter to five p.m., we all got the feeling that we wanted no visitors. We put a sign on the door to that effect and pulled the door to. Mum's breathing was changing a lot, getting shallower but still fast. Her feet got quite cold, and her hands were losing their warmth. Vicky, Dad, and Mark got closer to the bed and were all holding a hand, or touching her face. At 5:30, the phone rang - not exactly what we wanted... but it was Gyongyi on the line from Montreal, and we then realized how perfect this was. We told her the time was close, and held the phone up to Mum's ear so she could hear her sister speak to her; we then told Gyongyi to stay on the line and we put the phone on Mum's chest. Marika then took a few more spaced breaths and then simply stopped.

There was an unreal quality to the fact that what had happened had happened. Gyongyi's magnificent timing made it all seem so perfectly planned - she had raced home with the urgent feeling that she needed to call as soon as possible. Gyongyi and Marika's mother had saved them in the war by instinctively knowing to leave a building that was about to be bombed. Demonstrating more of that intuition, Dad had earlier in the week made a comment that 'no one can tell us it will happen at 5:24 on a Friday' - it in fact happened at 5:34 on Friday.

We had a good few cries and stayed with her for a period before we alerted the staff, which was very compassionate and supportive, telling us to take as much time as we wanted. We stayed for a bit but then decided to do what was inevitable and start cleaning the room, removing the dozens of cards and the pieces of Mum's art that had set the tone for her space.

For the past few days, I could not reconcile myself that the body in front of me was my mother - she did not have her character or her life force in it. I still gave her a goodbye kiss, as we all did, but felt that virtual hugs would be more abundant and forthcoming.

She was unbelievably tough to hang on as long as she did - everyone who knew her knows she was a tough cookie. But when it was time to let go, she did, surrounded by her immediate family. We are so sad to have her leave us but so grateful that her suffering doesn't need to go on, and that in fact at the end she was not suffering. She had been in far more pain when fighting the symptoms of the chemo - what landed her in hospital to begin with - and she recovered amazingly well from that process. Her bravery there was particularly noticeable - the symptoms were so horrific that I doubted whether I could have dealt with it with a fraction of her grace and fortitude.

Thank you all for being part of the journey. We have all appreciated your comments and good wishes, your contributions and kindness.

Serene Sunday

Quality family time continued over the weekend. David, Vicky, and Mark spent sunny time in some of Mum's favourite Victoria locations - Olive Olio's cafe (which is a great suntrap), Cattle Point, the Chinese Cemetery, and Willow's Beach.

We also went to Goward House to see the show that Studio Madrona, Mum's painting group, has dedicated to her. We were of course quite teary as we walked in to see a huge picture of Mum on the back wall announcing the dedication. All of her paintings had been placed together in a room to the side of the main exhibit hall, along with an easel featuring her bio. We sat with a couple of her friends who were visiting Goward House at the time and had a lovely chat.

For more information on the show, click here: http://www.goward-house.com/ArtShow2008-10.html

Click on the picture on the top left of the page to open up a page devoted to Mum, with her bio. Or click here: http://www.gowardhouse. com/ArtShowFile2008-10/Memorial.html

Inquiries are underway for the preparation of the Celebration of Life that we will hold in her honour. Stay tuned here for details shortly.

Also, we were informed via the blog that the flag will fly at half-mast for Marika at UNBC. If someone local could take a picture for us, we'd appreciate it.

Her obituary for the newspapers is being finalized and we will also be posting it here. We have decided upon suggesting that donations in her memory be made to Victoria Hospice at the Royal Jubilee Hospital in Victoria at http://www.victoriahospice.org/

Tuesday's News

Some updates from developments today:

- The date for Marika's Celebration of Life will be Saturday October 18th; it will take place at Goward House from 2 p.m. to 5 p.m.at http://www.gowardhouse.com/ . The space has a limited capacity, and so we will be asking all those wishing to attend to RSVP at marika.ainley@shaw.ca . We will fill you in on other details as they evolve.

- An obituary was posted on the Concordia University website at http://news.concordia.ca/notices/013438.shtml . As the page notes, a fuller obituary will be published in the October 9 issue of the Concordia Journal.

- We are awaiting pictures to be sent of the flags flown at half-mast at UNBC in Prince George - you can send them to mark@markainley.com . Thanks to Helen and the others who took them! We will be posting them here when they arrive.

- We'd also like to thank everyone for their generosity in showing their sympathy, and ask that in lieu of flowers donations can be made to Victoria Hospice Society, 1952 Bay Street, Victoria, V8R 1J8 or

http://www.victoriahospice.org/

UNBC Tribute

http://marikaainley.blogspot.ca/2008/10/unbc-tribute.html

Flags at UNBC flying at half-mast on September 29 in tribute to Marika.

And an online tribute at http://www.unbc.ca/womenstudies/ (scroll down)

One Week Later

Gyongyi put it right today. "The first everything is hard." It was one week today that Marika passed away. We all hard our eye on the time as it was approaching 5:34. First there was a chat with Vicky (who's in Vancouver recuperating from a mild cold) and then with Gyongyi. We had a drink to Mum - not the last, I'm sure.

Preparations are still underway for the Celebration of Life at Goward House, Saturday October 18 from 2 p.m. to 5 p.m. Please RSVP to marika. ainley@shaw.ca as space is regrettably limited - we're already at 50% capacity. Who could expect anything less than a cracking party where Marika is involved?

Online Obituary

The following slightly expanded obituary was posted online: http://www.legacy.com/EnhancedObit/EnhancedObit.aspx? PersonID=118190925

It was done a bit quickly - nature of the beast where these things are concerned - and we planned to expand it some more but when I tried again today it seemed to be locked. Will try again and hopefully will be able to add some other photos and details. There is a guestbook that can be signed as well.

Marvelous Madronas

http://marikaainley.blogspot.ca/2008/10/marvelous-madronas.html

The art group Mum belonged to, Studio Madrona, had their artists' reception this afternoon. It was a lovely if somewhat emotional visit - other people's emotion can bring out ours quite easily. They had added a few touches to the space at Goward House - lettering above the room where they had placed Mum's artwork, as well as a guest book especially for Marika and also a lovely portrait that Amy had spent all week preparing in time for today (photo to come later). We were so touched by everyone's kind words, loving thoughts, and concern.

Vicky and I looked over the downstairs space, which, while less homey than the upstairs, will make a great gallery and conversation space. We have a few great ideas planned...

Do be in touch if you plan to attend on October 18th - write to marika.ainley@shaw.ca.

Celebration of Life - Clarification

We have realized that when we stated that there was a limited space for Marika's Celebration of Life, some people may have chosen not to attend as a result. Please do not be put off by the fact that there is officially a restricted number. That number is 110 indoors at any given time, and since the Celebration is 3 hours long, we will certainly be able to accommodate everyone. We currently have 55 or so confirmed and are sure this number will climb - and we hope it will!

If you do wish to attend, please send an email to marika.ainley@shaw. ca . We need to be aware of numbers so that we can prepare appropriate catering and also to find contingencies, such as outdoor areas, if we do go over limit. The sooner we know, the more comfortable and enjoyable the event will be. (And let's all visualize lovely weather!)

Looking forward to seeing you on the 18th!

Tribute in the Concordia Journal

The following was published in the Concordia Journal, viewable at this link:

http://cjournal.concordia.ca/archives/20081009/in_memoriam_marika_marianne_gostztonyi_ainley_19372008.php

In Memoriam: Marika (Marianne) Gosztonyi Ainley
1937-2008

Colleagues, friends and former students were saddened by news that Marika Ainley passed away on September 26 after a battle with cancer.

Ainley began teaching at Concordia in 1988 and was the principal of the Simone de Beauvoir Institute from 1991 to 1995. She then served as professor and chair of women's studies at the University of Northern British Columbia. She continued to teach at UNBC until 2002 and became Professor Emeritus in 2005.

Among the many friends she made at Concordia, Susan Hoecker-Drysdale said this in a recent email: "She was not only a superb person, dear wife and mother, a highly creative artist and photographer, but a great friend to many many people, a dedicated mentor, teacher, researcher, administrator. She bridged the gap between the community and the academy, especially with Native women, in Montreal and British Columbia."

Hoecker-Drysdale contributed to the book Ainley edited in 1989. *Against the Odds: Essays on Canadian Women in Science* was one of two books Ainley published on the history of science in Canada with Véhicule Press.

Another colleague from the Simone de Beauvoir Institute, Barbara Meadowcroft, added, "Marika had a gift for friendship. Through her several moves, her circle of friends just kept growing. She kept in touch with all of us in Montreal and never forgot a birthday."

Ainley's varied career began in her native Hungary where she studied industrial chemistry in the '50s. In Montreal, she registered in English and French literature at Sir George Williams University and earned her B.A. in 1964. She then earned both her M.A. and Ph.D. studying the history of science, and eventually returned to teach at Concordia.

While committed to unearthing the often-neglected history of women in the pure sciences, Ainley pursued varied interests. She studied pottery in Montreal in the 1960s and turned to painting in recent years. Her work is currently being exhibited at a gallery in Victoria. She was an avid birder and a lifelong naturalist.

Ainley passed away peacefully in Victoria surrounded by her husband David, daughter Vicky, and son Mark, with her sister Gyongyi on the phone. Those who would like to know more about Ainley and her family can visit marikaainley.blogspot.com/

A celebration of Ainley's life is being organized on October 18, 2 to 5 p.m. at Goward House in Victoria. A Montreal celebration of her life will be held at a later date: watch news@concordia or the Simone de Beauvoir Institute website for details. Donations in her name can be made to Victoria Hospice Society, 1952 Bay Street, Victoria.

Celebration of Life

Marika's Celebration of Life is taking place this Saturday, October 18, at Goward House in Victoria.

http://www.gowardhouse.com/contact.html . The hours of the celebration are 2:00 to 5:00 p.m. It is not a 'service' per se so you don't need to arrive early in order to get a 'seat' - feel free to arrive for 2:00 p.m. or whenever is convenient, keeping in mind that there will be a few short speeches around 3:00 p.m. or so. There will be a continuous slideshow, art display of Marika's work, and displays of photos taken throughout Marika's life.

We are looking forward to seeing all of the friends who are able to attend to celebrate our dear Marika.

Celebration of Life Photos

Some photos from today's wonderful Celebration of Life. More photos and an overview to follow.

http://marikaainley.blogspot.ca/2008/10/celebration-of-life-photos.html

The Celebration of Life

We awoke the morning of Saturday October 18 to a beautiful sunny day - exactly what we had hoped for when we planned the event. Vicky and Mark headed in early to continue the set-up in the basement at Goward House that Vicky, David, and the Madronas had started the day before. On the drive there, as the car turned a corner near Goward House, a bald eagle flew overhead - and the first painting Mark noticed upon entering the space was one Marika had made of a bald eagle. A good one, we all thought!

The downstairs space looked lovely - it really is a stark room ordinarily, but with the photo displays, paintings, and flowers all over, it was thoroughly transformed. We set up the DVD player so that the slideshow could play on the large screen. The caterers (Cook's Day Off, who did a wonderful job) showed up at 1:00 p.m. and started setting up, and everything started to fall into place.

Some people started arriving before the 2:00 p.m. start, and then they just kept on coming in. We had several people from out of town - from Vancouver, Prince George, Montreal, and Washington DC. Marika's sister Gyongyi was present with her husband Jerry and children Randi and Stephen. The room started filling up very quickly and we got to speak with lots of people.

We had to crank the music quite loudly to get people's attention at 3:15 for the start of the speeches. Everyone was very much involved in conversation and seemed to be having a good time. Dad went first, and delivered a moving speech. He had been nervous that he would not be able to get through it, but he did marvelously, adding a few spontaneous touches (and a funny Freudian slip). Then Gyongyi shared briefly about childhood with her sister and how she misses her best friend. Mary Baldwin, a friend of over 40 years, gave a very comprehensive overview of Marika's academic life and accomplishments. And then Annelie Dominik crowned the speeches with a glorious tribute to Marika the artist, ending with a beautiful image of a Hungarian Firecracker letting off an "explosion of energy shooting up into the skies, transforming into an array of glittering stars and a rainbow of color, then descending and sprinkling us all with a little magic."

The party continued fully despite the fact that the main food from Cook's Day Off had been gobbled up! They had seriously underestimated the vibrant appetites of Mum's friends! Fortunately we had ordered some Hungarian apple squares from Mum's friend Katy, and these certainly were welcome additions to the menu.

We were happy that Dr. Wild from Hebden Bridge came by - he arrived in the middle of the speeches and was looking around very intently, taking in the life of a woman he had only known as a patient in hospital. He said that he had had to walk half a mile down the road because of all the cars of attendees - and this was apparently not a Yorkshire exaggeration! Vicky tried to get out to take a picture but with all of the social interactions that spontaneously popped up she didn't get one - so if anyone did get a picture, please send it along!

Near the end of the party, Vicky and Mark presented each member of the Madrona art group with a paintbrush from Mum's collection. It was a lovely way for us to gift her dear friends with something meaningful that they could use.

The three hours flew by and it was a really wonderful party. Of course, more than one person said that they wished Marika had been there - but she certainly was in spirit, and she was the glue that bound everyone together that sunny October afternoon, and who continues to be a part of the lives of countless people. Thank you to all those who attended, and to those who were unable to attend but sent their wishes. Another celebration was taking place in Prince George, and one is scheduled for November 9th at Concordia University in Montreal.

December 4, 2008

http://marikaainley.blogspot.ca/2008/12/december-4-2008.html (for photos)

Today would have been Marika's 71st birthday. At this time last year, the family was in Hawaii on our first birthday vacation trip. We certainly could not have imagined that it would be the last time we would celebrate David's, Mark's, and Marika's birthdays all together.

We decided some time ago that we would all spend Marika's birthday in Victoria, and had more recently discussed whether it would be an ideal time to spread her ashes. She had asked for it to be done at Cattle Point, a beautiful spot by the water in Victoria. We were uncertain if the weather would cooperate, and yet, as was the case with her Celebration of Life, conditions were ideal.

We arrived at Cattle Point just in time for the 7:49 sunrise. Its bright red tones were reminiscent of Marika herself. The wind had not yet picked up but there was a bit of a breeze by the time we had walked along the grass and reached the edge of the water.

The urn that we had purchased weighed a ton, so instead we brought the contents along in one of the pots that Mum had made in her pottery phase in the 70s. We decided that we would each take turns scattering some ashes, and that at the end the three of us would do some more together. David started off, then Mark, and then Vicky, before the three of us came together for the last bit.

As we walked back to the car, there was a brisker breeze, and the sun was brighter. We slowly drove off to have breakfast at Rosie's Diner, one of Marika's favourite places, and to continue spending the rest of her birthday together.

Still Influential at UNBC

Jennifer Swennumson, a former student and friend of Marika's, submitted an application to graduate studies at UNBC, where Marika had headed the Women's Studies department for several years. She listed Marika as her referee, giving this explanation:

Marika was to be my strongest reference. I knew her for many years personally and academically. Unfortunately before I was to submit my graduate application, she passed away suddenly. It is my wish to still have her as one of my referees as I know she would have wanted this, and it is partially my intention to honour an incredibly gifted woman who was vital to UNBC. In one of our many conversations, Marika told me she would be the first individual to be my reference for graduate studies. To quote her, "You have a brilliant mind, Jennifer. It is time to enroll in graduate studies. If you do not do it, I will never forgive you. Academically, you are one of the strongest women I have seen and it is time to use your gift...your brilliant mind." Marika Ainley, Winter 2008

Jennifer was accepted, and awarded a grant to assist with her studies.

Thank you, Jennifer, for sharing this story.

One year ago

(photos at http://marikaainley.blogspot.ca/2009/09/one-year-ago. html)

Where does time go? It is almost inconceivable that a year should have passed since Marika died. Her cousin Franci wrote to us today, saying, "Years go by, now there's one that has passed, 365 days and many heart beats. We think very much of you, especially this day." Certainly we have all been thinking of Marika a lot this year.

We had decided to spread some more of her ashes this morning at English Bay, near where Vicky and Mark live. It is a beautiful beach right in downtown Vancouver, along which Mum and Dad would walk when they visited.

We woke up relatively early (though not quite as early as Mum might have) and headed over to the beach before sunrise. There were already several people out, jogging, walking, feeding the birds (Mum would have disapproved of the latter).

We found a quiet stretch of beach and went right up to the water. The waves were coming in at a good speed, but were very shallow. We each took a turn scattering some ashes into the water.

We enjoyed the view for a few more moments, and then went off to have breakfast. We've had some messages and phone calls from friends and relatives, and will be thinking of Marika lots more today...

Two years later

Once again, September 26th has come and we are stunned when we consider that it is two years since Marika left us. Where does the time go? It scarcely seems possible that more than two years have passed since we saw her in peak form, filling a room with her presence, humour, and intellect.

David came to Vancouver to spend the weekend with Vicky and Mark so that we could be together on this anniversary. We know that she would have been happy for us to be with each other and thinking of her fondly. We were touched by the cards, emails, and Facebook postings by friends and relatives, and enjoyed some good food and drink that we know she would have appreciated.

Good news on two fronts:

We are closer to finishing a tribute volume featuring the entire content of this blog, with additional testimonials and photographs.

Marika's final manuscript is almost ready for publication! There had been some revisions that were needed which she could not complete due to her illness. Her friends Geoffrey and Marelene Rayner-Canhem have made the necessary revisions and we received confirmation from UBC Press that the book is in the final stages of preparation required prior to publication. We are so grateful and excited that Marika's hard work will not be silenced by her untimely departure, and express our sincere thanksto those who helped to make this possible. Updates will be posted as the timeline becomes more defined.

The three of us will be going to Four Corners in the American Southwest, a location David and Marika had wanted to go to but didn't on their few visits to the area. We are looking forward to making a family holiday to this area that Marika loved so much.

With thanks and love for your thoughts and wishes,

David, Vicky, and Mark

(photo at http://marikaainley.blogspot.ca/2010/09/two-years-later. html)

Marsha Ross, In Memory of Marika

Marika standing beside her artwork. Aug. 4, 2006

My other self, in progress,
Sept. 2006

A Meeting Place

Guestbook Art and Letters

DREAMING OF COUNTESS MARIKA
Jacqueline Baldwin

Marika: I had to write this dream down before it fades. You looked so lovely in your sage green and sable Chanel suit in this dream I had about you, and we were all having such a good time!

We are in a restaurant talking and talking after some workers have come to clear the tables. The atmosphere is more like that of a potluck supper than a public restaurant. The women who have organized the evening ask us to move to an anteroom, which has counters on one side and a row of cupboards on the other.

Marika, elegant red haired Hungarian who often speaks with a Yorkshire accent mixed with Montreal idiom and peppered with charming emphasis on the first syllable of English words, is sitting with her long legs crossed, wearing a sable and sage green Chanel suit, holding forth.

"Zeze bugghers," she says, "now they tell me they don't like my political beliefs and George Boosch, of all people, he has declared that I am to be known in future as a public nuisance!"

She shakes her head in amazement; she cannot believe that George Bush has dared to disagree with her. "He of all people is calling me a nuisance!" she exclaims to all of us who are standing around, sipping our wine, trying to stay out of the way of the people who are clearing the large dining tables where we have just finished having dinner.

Marika has a new haircut, more sleek and a little bit longer, but still the same golden shade. A woman who is in charge of the clearing-up asks her if she would mind moving over to the other side of the room, where the rest of us stand, leaning against the four foot high row of cupboards. One woman says: "I would like it if George Bush called me a nuisance, I would wear it as a badge of honour." "I will too, definitely, I will, but first we need to discuss what lies behind this statement that has no basis in fact," says Marika, and goes on with her tirade against blind politicians who have butter for brains and lead their followers from one disaster to another, destroying everything in sight en route.

I say to Marika: "Bet you can't leap onto the top of this counter over here, it's way higher than the one you are sitting on." She looks at me with one eyebrow raised as she slides from the lower counter, walks across the room, grins and says "Oh, really? Just watch me." Turning her back toward the cupboards, she bends her elbows back and upwards and leans her hands on the top of the cupboards. With one graceful move she lands on that high counter, crosses her legs and says indignantly: "A *nuisance*. I am not just a *nuisance*, but I have become a *declared* nuisance."

Ten women stand there laughing and applauding her. For a moment, Marika looks puzzled. Leaping backwards onto high counters is nothing remarkable to her. Besides, she is waiting for us to begin discussion, comment, reaction to George Bush calling her a *nuisance*.

But we are all too busy appreciating her, and laughing with delight after observing her latest achievement: the agility to slide gracefully off one counter, cross the room, and leap gazelle-like onto a higher perch, without ever once having stopped talking.

(This was written in 2001, but we all need to smile again.)

Maureen Doyle, Guestbook Art, 2008. "Marika, You are our heart, our centre. Your energy and creativity will endure."

Dana Hearne

Dear Marianne,

I chose this poem for you because I love its subversive quality and know you would love it too. From one star-gazer and fire-eater to another, with love, Dana.

It's a Woman's World by Eavan Boland*

(* Note: due to copyright rules, this poem and the following two poems cannot be printed in their entirety. See references.)

Please find below an excerpt:

(1) Our way of life
has hardly changed
since a wheel first
whetted a knife.

(12) But appearances
still reassure:
That woman there,
craned to the starry mystery

(13) is merely getting a breath
of evening air,
while this one here –
her mouth

(14) a burning plume –
she's no fire-eater,
just my frosty neighbour
coming home.

Katherine Waters

These two poems spoke Marika to me. Adrienne Rich's "Planetarium" begins in thinking of Caroline Herschel, a then-relatively obscure woman scientist, a pioneering astronomer known chiefly for helping her more famous brother William. The poem swirls outward in its explorations, encountering lost and transgressive women, and through recovering them also moves inward, recovering and transforming the woman poet-speaker herself into an identity beyond the personal. Seeing in a changed way, she becomes a receptor for the energy of these past women and a transmitter of that energy to us.

Below is an excerpt:

Planetarium, by Adrienne Rich*

Thinking of Caroline Herschel (1750—1848)
astronomer, sister of William; and others.

(Line 35) I have been standing all my life in the
direct path of a battery of signals
the most accurately transmitted most
untranslatable language in the universe

(Line 42) taken   I am an instrument in the shape
of a woman trying to translate pulsations
into images   for the relief of the body
and the reconstruction of the mind.

To me, this poem personifies two impulses of artistic creativity: the celestial-seeking, music-aspiring, urge to liberation, seen also in the painting Marika gave to Susan and John, with its swirling dark blue night sky; and the earth-rooted, drawing strength from daylight and the sun, seen in the wonderful reds and browns of the painting she gave to me inspired by the Madrone tree grove of coastal B.C. As a poem of the 1950s it genderizes the two impulses as masculine and feminine, the artist as androgynous.

Bartok and the Geranium, by Dorothy Livesay*

Below is an excerpt:

(3) She's daylight
He is dark
She's heaven-held breath
He storms and crackles
Spits with hell's own spark.

(4) Yet in this room, this moment now
These together breathe and be:
She, essence of serenity,
He is a mad intensity
Soars beyond sight…

(5) And when he's done, he's out:
She leans a lip against the glass
And preens herself in light

"Cheeky crows at "Cattle Point""

One of Marika's favourite spots, and mine!
I see you everytime I go there!
Alice Webster

"Cheeky Crows at Cattle Point." One of Marika's favourite spots and mine! I see you everytime I go there. Guestbook art. Alice Webster

"I'm hoping this little watercolour sketch reminds you of cocktail hours enjoyed in nature with Marika... somewhere in the world! As I painted it, I could hear her say "More colour, just a little bit here, or there perhaps." She was a very colourful person, and will be sadly missed by us, especially at Studio Madrona."Bonny Myers

Marika, by Marsha Ross, Guestbook 2008

Winter is a sketch,

Spring, an acrylic,

summer an oil painting,

But the autumn; is a mosaic of them all.

Just as you were, dear Marika,

a multifaceted individual of talents:

Chemist, Naturalist, Professor, Author

Artist, Friend, Wife & Mother...

Filled with an inner glow,

an eternal brightness of being;

all of us have benefitted

From the joy of knowing you.

You will be forever missed.

Kate Millar Newman

I am so pleased you are honouring Marianne. She was wonderful as a teacher and a colleague and so supportive of all of us. She always gave credit to the work we did and wanted us to succeed. She seemed to believe our progress would enrich her reputation.

When I married Frank and came to Victoria I was delighted to meet her again.

I was so sorry she was sick and I feel we lost a great mind and a lovely person.

Please tell Marianne's family I am privileged to have known her and to have worked with her. She was a lady and a scholar and the world is poorer without her.

A Letter Between Friends

Hi Katherine (Waters),

I successfully nominated Marika for a Long Term Service Award this year - thought you'd like to read the citation.

Her sister was at the AGM to accept the award & expressed her pleasure to have Marika so honored. I didn't get a chance to speak with her afterwards.

Best regards, Audrey (Speck)

BIRD PROTECTION QUEBEC
2008 LONG TERM SERVICE AWARDS

The Long Term Service Awards are discretionary awards given most years in recognition of members who have contributed significantly to the smooth running of Bird Protection Quebec over many years and are now reducing active involvement.

Marika Ainley (Posthumously)
The official citation reads:

"Marika Ainley was a long-time member of Bird Protection Quebec. Born in Hungary she came to Montreal in the 1970s and joined Bird Protection Quebec soon after. Marika became a Director of the Society and served as Chair of the Research Committee from 1982 to 1992. She also served on the Education Committee for many years and sat on the editorial board of *Tchébec*. When the rare bird hot line was in danger of collapse she took it over and ran it well for many years. Marika often said that one of her proudest achievements was the instigation of the early morning field trips to Westmount Summit, now dedicated to the memory of Jim Houghton. Marika moved with her family to Prince George, B. C. in 1995 and retired to Victoria. Throughout her days in western Canada she kept up her contacts with her many friends in Bird Protection Quebec. Marika Ainley was a significant force within BPQ during her long residence in Montreal. She was also an active promoter of the history of science specifically Canadian ornithology. She obtained her Ph.D. from McGill University in 1985 with a dissertation entitled *From Natural History to Avian Biology: Canadian Ornithology 1860-1950*. She also authored a book on the Canadian ornithologist William Rowan, and contributed many papers to scholarly journals on Canadian science, particularly ornithology, as well as on women in science and the environment.

Bird Protection Quebec posthumously recognizes Marika Ainley with a Long Term Service Award in honour of her significant contributions to our Society."

Geoff and Marelene Rayner-Canham, Eds.

Creating Complicated Lives: Women and Science at English-Canadian Universities, 1880–1980, Marianne Gosztonyi Ainley

"There was a special meaning for us to undertake this task. Over 20 years ago, we had written an account of the life and work of Harriet Brooks. (*Harriet Brooks: Pioneer Nuclear Scientist*, Montreal: McGill Queen's Press, 1992) We had submitted it for support for publication and one of the reviewers was Marika. She extolled the importance of the work but added gently that it suffered from a major flaw - that we had written it in the style of natural scientists, without context. She pleaded with the granting agency to make a special exception and, instead of turning the project down, to put the grant application on hold until, with her advice, we could write a contextualized version. To their great credit, the agency did 'bend their own rules' and do this. The revised work was subsequently published by McGill-Queen's U.P. So our work on Marika's book was, in some ways, a repayment of her own generosity towards us. We think that Brook's book also established our credibility with McGill-Queen's U.P."

73rd Canadian Chemical Conference, Halifax, N.S. July 1990. Mary E. Baldwin, Geoff Rarner-Canham, Marelene Rayner-Canham, unknown, Marianne G. Ainley, Bertrum H. Macdonald, Margaret-Ann Armour

Book Review by Michelle Hoffman

Historical Studies in Education / Revue d'histoire de l'éducation

"These last four chapters consist primarily of approximately fifty short vignettes, usually one to two pages long, of Canadian women scientists whose biographies she unearthed in the course of her extensive research. Ainley's decision to use a biographical, qualitative approach flows out of her choice of analytical lens, namely, "life course change," which is defined as "a biographical/geographical approach that follows women's lives across space and time." One of her aims is to avoid comparing women's working lives to a "male-stream" career norm. As a result, Ainley casts a wide net in her research, making sure to include often overlooked roles, including "in/visible assistants" such as laboratory technicians. She takes pains not to overgeneralize within her categories of analysis and repeatedly points to the variety of women's individual experiences, whether married, single, mothers, or childless. In framing her story, Ainley continually draws on a broad range of secondary literature, evincing a deep familiarity with feminist scholarship spanning the past four decades."

Book Review by Ruby Heap

The Canadian Historical Review

"*Creating Complicated Lives* succeeds in its efforts to reveal the complex and dynamic relationships between women and science in Canadian universities. Those profiled in the book are far from a monolithic and unilateral group: they are single, married or divorced, with or without children, immigrant or Canadian-born, part-time or full-time, some focusing less on research and more on teaching or administrative duties, with others embracing causes such as feminism and pacifism. These women worked in different disciplines and institutions at different times, hence the wide range of rules and practices across labs, departments, faculties, and universities. Such diversity certainly calls for nuanced discussions, which must also take into account the evolving status of women in society and of science as a profession."

Bamboo Watercolour

Timeline

This is not meant to be a comprehensive account of all of Marika's work, nor a list of the many people she knew. Her complete Curriculum Vitae can be found in the archives at the University of Northern British Columbia in Prince George, BC. Instead, the following is an interwoven timeline containing family, friends, colleagues and personal events along with professional ones. Older scholarship on scientists has stated that work and family must be separate entities, and for a person to be successful, one entity should not be allowed to complicate the other. Marika would strongly disagree with this statement, especially when commenting on the lives of women scientists, who were often trying to balance it all.

Marika, 1959, Montreal, Q.C.

Living Life Forward

1937 - Born in Budapest, Hungary, on December 4

1956 - Obtains a Diploma of Industrial Chemistry, at Petrik Lajos Poly-techical College of Chemistry, Budapest, Hungary

1956 - Escapes to Sweden during the Hungarian uprising and then settles in Montreal

1957 - Marries George Marton, whom she knew in Hungary, but they had escaped separately. They later met again in Montreal.

1958-1959 - Works as a laboratory technician, at Chemaco Co., Montreal

1959-1963 - Works as a laboratory technician for Imperial Tobacco Company, Montreal

1962 - Her sister Gyöngyi, five years younger, moves to Montreal

1963 - Birth of their daughter Vicky

1964 - Marianne and George divorce and go their separate ways

1964 - Completes a B.A. as a part time evening student in English/French literature, and psychology, at Sir George Williams University, Montreal, (later renamed Concordia)

1964-1966 - Works as a Research Assistant in the Immunology Laboratory, at Queen Mary Veterans' Hospital, in Montreal

1966 - Marries David Ainley, a high school teacher for the Protestant School Board in Montreal

1966-1969 - Works at the Department of Chemistry of Loyola College, Montreal, as a research assistant for Thomas Nogrády, Ph.D.

1969 - Is accepted into a master's program in anthropology, but post-pones her entrance

1969 - Birth of their son, Mark, in Montreal

1972 - Joins American Ornithological Union, acts as a member of their Centennial Committee in 1982-1983

1973 - 1995 - Acts a Director for the Province of Quebec Society for the Protection of Birds, and member of the Editorial Board, Tchébec, from 1977 to 1987

1974 - Returns to work at Department of Chemistry of Loyola College, becomes a laboratory instructor for General Chemistry. Meets Michael Hogben, head of Interdisciplinary Studies at Loyola. He suggests History of Science as a field for academic study

1978 - Enrolls in Institut d'Histoire et de Sociololitique at Université de Montréal

1979 - Completes a Certificate in Ornithology, at the Laboratory of Ornithology, Cornell University, Ithaca, NY

1979-1980 - Becomes a Research Assistant in History of Science at Concordia University, Montreal with Susan Sheets Pyenson, Ph.D. for "The Analysis of Sir John William Dawson's Correspondence with 19th Century Naturalists"

1980 - Graduates with an M.S., thesis entitled "La professionalization de l'ornithologie Américaine 1970-1979" with Lewis Pyenson, Ph.D as her supervisor. Receives a doctoral fellowship from FCAC Quebec and moves to McGill University to complete her Ph.D. in history and philosophy of science with Maxwell J. Dunbar

1980-1981- Becomes a Research Assistant in History of Science at the University of Montreal for Yakov Rabkin, Ph.D, Principal Investigator in "History of Infrared Spectroscopy"

1985 - Graduates from McGill with a Ph.D. dissertation titled "From Natural History to Avian Biology: Canadian Ornithology, 1860-1950"

1985 - Is awarded an 'independent researcher' grant from the Canadian Social Sciences and Humanities Research Council (SSHRC), and begins work on a scientific biography of William Rowan, a British-trained ornithologist who came to Canada to establish the Department of Zoology at the University of Alberta

1984-1985 - Is awarded a small grant from the Canadian Institute for the Advancement of Women to work on "Canadian Women Natural Scientists: A Pilot Project"

1985-1986 - Receives a postdoctoral fellowship for work on "History of Canadian Women in Science" in the History Department of McGill University

1985 - Curates (with E. MacLean), "The Bicentennial of J. J. Audubon" exhibition, Blacker-Wood Library, McGill University

1985-1990 - Contributes to "The Quebec Breeding Bird Atlas, Environment Canada, 1985-90"

1986-1992 - Is awarded two SSHRC strategic grants for "Women and Scientific Work" as an independent scholar (meaning she still did not have as institutional affiliation)

1986 - Meets Arpi Hammalian, then the Principal of the Simone de Beauvoir Institute at Concordia University, and becomes a research fellow at the Institute, which housed the Women's Studies Program

1988 - Begins teaching at the Simone de Beauvoir Institute and develops a course on "Historical and Contemporary Perspectives of Women, Science, and Technology"

1988 - Becomes an Associate Scholar of History of Science Society (U.S)

1988 - Becomes an Advisory Editor, Scientia Canadensis, a scholarly journal on Canadian History of Science, and in 2002 becomes a Member of the Editorial Board

1988-1989 - Organizes a Session on the History of Canadian Biology, 6th Kingston Conference of the Canadian Science and Technology Historical Association, 1988-89.

1990 - Attends Carleton University as a Visiting Scholar in the Women's Studies Program

1990 - After soliciting and editing a series of essays on Canadian women and their scientific activities, organizes and edits "Despite the Odds: Essays on Canadian Women and Science (published by Véhicule: Montreal)

1990-1993 - Curates "Canadian Achievements of Science" a historical exhibition, Concordia University Science Exhibition

1990 - Is a Referee for Revue d'histoire de l'Amérique française

1991-1995 - Becomes Principal of the Simone de Beauvoir Institute and Director and Associate Professor of Women's Studies at Concordia University. Is a co-investigator on an SSHRC strategic grant on "Women Engineers Within and Outside the Profession"

1991-1993 - Chairs the Scientific Programme Committee, 8th Kingston Conference of the Canadian Science and Technology Historical Association

1991 - Organizes the Symposium, "The History of Canadian Ornithology," American Ornithologists' Union Annual Meeting, Montreal

1991 - Organizes the "History of Canadian Ornithology" exhibition Redpath Museum, McGill University

1992 - Organizes the Symposium, "The Laboratory in the Field Sciences," 2nd Joint British-North American Conference on the History of Science, Toronto, 1992.

1993 - Organizes and Chairs "Feminist Scientific Biography," History of Science Society Annual Meeting, Santa Fe, New Mexico

1993 – Accepts first graduate student, Ernestine (Tina) Crossfield, M.A., S.I.P., School of Graduate Studies, Concordia University, 1993-95

1993-1999 - Becomes President of the Canadian Science and Technology Historical Association

1993 - Authors *Restless Energy – A Biography of William Rowan, 1891-1957* (Véhicule Press: Montreal)

1993-1999 - Becomes President of the Canadian Science and Technology Historical Association

1994-1998 - Acts a Member of the Editorial Advisory Board, Science and Technology in Canadian History: A Bibliography of Secondary Works

1994 - David Ainley retires from teaching for more then 30 years for the Protestant School Board of Greater Montreal.

1995 - Becomes Professor and Chair of Women's Studies at the new University of Northern British Columbia (UNBC)

1996-2003 - Supervises more than 15 graduate students at UNBC who begin successful professional careers.

1997 - Curates "Canadian achievements in science" photo exhibition, UNBC Works

1997 - Begins to actively pursue painting and artwork

1998-2004 - Joins as a Member of the UNBC Arts Council

1998-1999 - Chairs the Curriculum Committee, Women's Studies/Gender Studies at UNBC

1998 - Organizes "Research on Canadian Women in Science and Engineering in Canada: Historical and Contemporary Perspectives," Panel Discussion, 98 Congress, Ottawa

1998 - UNBC community member, organizes and participates on the jury committee, "Other Eyes: Art, Racism and Stereotypes" 2nd annual exhibition, UNBC Arts Council and Prince George Art Gallery, 1998.

1999 - UNBC community member, organizing committee, "Body Image" exhibition at the Prince George Art Gallery

1999-2000 - Is elected President, Canadian Women's Studies Association

1996-1999 - Is a Member of the Selection Committee, Canadian Science and Engineering Hall of Fame, National Museum of Science and Technology

1995-1998 - Referees for publications: *Isis: an international review devoted to the history of science and its cultural influences, Hannah Foundation for the History of Medicine, Social Science and Humanities Research Council of Canada, Alternatives*

1993-1995 - Is a Member of the Ontario Science Centre "Whose Science Is It?" Project Advisory Panel

2000 - Becomes a Distinguished Visitor, Centre for Social Science Research at Central Queensland University, Rockhampton, Australia

2001 - Becomes a Visiting Scholar at the Institute for the Study of Gender at Auckland University, New Zealand

2001- Is awarded a SSHRC grant on "Re-explorations: New Perspectives on Gender, Environment, and Transfer of Knowledge in Nineteenth and Twentieth Century Canada and Australia

2001 - Is awarded Professor Emeritus from Concordia University, retroactive to 1995

2002 - Takes mandatory retirement from UNBC

2003 – Is a Visiting Scholar at the Australian National University, Canberra, and Central Queensland University

2004 – Moves to Victoria, BC with her husband David Ainley

2004 - Joins the Madrona Art Studio in Victoria, and meets many new artists friends

2005 - Is awarded Professor Emerita from UNBC

2005 - Diagnosed with breast cancer

2006 - Becomes a Visiting Scholar at Alcoa Research centre for Stronger Communities at Curtin University in Perth, Western Australia

2008 - Reads her first reviews on the manuscript "Overlooked Dimensions: Women and Scientific Work at Canadian Universities, 1884-1980

2008 - Dies on September 26 in Victoria, BC

Only in Australia

Publications (Last to First)

Books

Overlooked dimensions: women and scientific work at Canadian universities, 1884-1980. Published posthumously as *Creating Complicated Lives: Women and Science at English-Canadian Universities, 1880-1980*, eds. Marelene Rayner-Canham and Geoff Rayner-Canham. McGill-Queens University Press, 2012.

Restless Energy   a Biography of   William Rowan, 1891-1957. 368 pp. bibl., index. Véhicule Press, 1993.

Despite The Odds: Essays on Canadian Women and Science. Edited and with an essay and a bibliography by Marianne Gosztonyi Ainley. 452 pp., bibl., index. Véhicule Press, 1990.

Niva Rowan, Marika, David, and Julia Rowan celebratiing the launch of "Restless Energy," 1993.

Chapters in Books

"Gendered Careers: Women Science Educators at Anglo-Canadian Universities, 1920-1980." in Historical Identities: The professoriate in Canada. eds. Paul Stortz and Lisa Panayotidis, 248-270. Toronto: University of Toronto Press, 2006.

"Science, Environment, and Women's Lives: Integrating Teaching and Research." in Teaching as Activism: Equity Meets Environmentalism. eds. Peggy Tripp and Linda Muzzin , 107-117. Montreal and Kingston: McGill-Queens University Press, 2005.

"Women and Science," in Bob Hesketh and Chris Hackett, eds. Canada: Confederation to the Present: A History. [Web Site]. Edmonton: Chinook Multimedia, 2001.

"Norah Toole (1906-1990): Scientist and Social Activist." in Framing our Past: Women in Canada in the Twentieth Century, eds. Kate O'Rourke, Loran McLean and Sharon Cook, 308-310. Montreal-Kingston: McGill-Queens Press, 2001.

"Les femmes dans les sciences au Canada: Y-a-t-il une division sexuelle du travail?" In Femme et Sciences, eds. Lucie Dumais and Veronique Boudreau, 1-15. Ottawa: University of Ottawa Press, 1997.

"Science in Canada's `Backwoods': Catharine Parr Traill." In Natural Eloquence: Women Reinscribe Science, eds. Barbara T. Gates and Ann B. Shteir, 79-97. Madison: University of Wisconsin Press, 1997.

"Soaring to New Heights: Changes in the Life Course of Mabel McIntosh." In Great Dames, eds. Elspeth Cameron and Janice Dickin, 259-281. Toronto: University of Toronto Press 1997.

"Allan Brooks (1869-1946)." In A Biographical Dictionary of North American Environmentalists, eds. Keir B. Sterling et al., 117-19. Greenwoods, Ct.: Greenwood Press, 1997.

"W. H. Mousley (1865-1949)." In A Biographical Dictionary of North American Environmentalists, eds. Keir B. Sterling et al., 561-64. Greenwood, Ct.: Greenwood Press, 1997.

"Percy A. Taverner (1875-1947)."In A Biographical Dictionary of North

American Environmentalists, eds. Keir B. Sterling et al., 767-79. Greenwood Ct.: Greenwood Press, 1997.

"Lewis McIver Terrill (1878-1968)." In A Biographical Dictionary of North American Environmentalists, ed. Keir B. Sterling et al., 770-72. Greenwood Ct.: Greenwood Press, 1997.

"Foreword." In A Devotion to Their Science: Pioneer Women of Radioactivity, eds. Marelene Rayner-Canham and Geoffrey Rayner-Canham, eds., xiii-xiv. Montreal: McGill University Press, 1997.

"The Eastern Screech-owl." In Atlas of the Breeding Birds of Quebec, 586-89. Ottawa and Quebec: Canadian Wildlife Service, 1996.

"Marriage and Scientific Work in Twentieth-Century Canada: the Berkeleys in Marine Biology and the Hoggs in Astronomy." In Creative Couples in the Sciences, eds., Helena Pycior, Nancy Slack and Pnina Abir-Am, 143-55. New Brunswick, N.J.: Rutgers University Press, 1996.

"The Emergence of Canadian Ornithology--An Historical Overview to 1950." In Contributions to the History of North American Ornithology, eds., W. E. Davis & Jerome A. Jackson, 283-302. Boston: Nuttall Ornithological Club Press, 1995.

"Foreword: Thomas McIlwraith (1824-1903) and the Birds of Ontario." pp. In Ornithology in Ontario, eds., Martin McNicholl and J. Cranmer-Byng, viii-xiii. Whitby, Ont.: Hawk Owl Publishing, 1994.

"Margaret H. Mitchell (1901-1988)" In Ornithology in Ontario, eds., Martin McNicholl and J. Cranmer-Byng, 185-188. Whitby, Ont.: Hawk Owl Publishing, 1994.

"Last in the Field? Canadian Women Natural Scientists, 1815 1965." In Despite the Odds. Essays on Canadian Women and Science, ed., Marianne Gosztonyi Ainley, 25-62. Montreal: Véhicule Press, 1990.

"William Rowan and the Experimental Approach in Ornithology." In Proceedings of the 19th International Ornithological Congress, Ottawa (1986), ed. Henri Ouellet, 2737-45. Ottawa: The University of Ottawa Press, 1988.

"Field Work and Family: North American Women Ornithologists, 1900 1950." *In Uneasy Careers and Intimate Lives: Women in Science 1789 1979.* eds., Pnina Abir-Am and Dorinda Outram, 60 76. New Brunswick, N. J.:Rutgers University Press, 1987.

Articles in Refereed Journals

"Une nouvelle optique concernant la recherche sur l'histoire des femmes canadiennes et les sciences."Recherches feministes 15, 1 (2002): 93-111.

"'Despite the Odds' Revisited: Reflections on Canadian Women and Science." Simone de Beauvoir Review 18/19 (1999-2000):85-100.

"Mabel F. Timlin, 1891-1976: A woman economist in the world of men." Atlantis: A Women's Studies Journal 23, 2 (1999): 28-38.

"Women's Work in Geology: An Historical Perspective on Gender Division in Canadian Science." Geoscience Canada 21, no. 3 (1995): 139-141.

"Louise de Kiriline Lawrence (1894-1992) and the World of Nature: A Tribute." The Canadian Field-Naturalist 108, no. 1 (1994): 111-117.

"Canadian Women's Contributions to Chemistry, 1900-1970." Canadian Chemical News 46, no. 4 (1994): 16-18.

"A Woman of Integrity: Kathleen Gough's `Career' in Canada." Anthropologica 35, no. 2 (June 1993): 235-243.

"'Women's Work' in Canadian Chemistry," Canadian Woman Studies 13, no. 2 (Winter 1993): 43-46.

"In Memoriam: Louise de Kiriline Lawrence, 1894-1992," Auk 109 (1992): 909-910.

"A Select Few: Women and the National Research Council of Canada, 1916-1991." Scientia Canadensis 15, no. 2 (1991): 105-116.

"William Rowan, 1891-1957." Bulletin of the Canadian Society of Zoologists 22 (January 1991): 33-35.

"In Memoriam: Margaret Howell Mitchell, 1901-1988." Auk 107 (1990): 601-602.

"Rowan vs. Tory - Conflicting Views of Scientific Research in Canada, 1920 1935," Scientia Canadensis 12, no.1 (1988): 3-21.

"William Rowan: Canada's First Avian Biologist," Picoides 1 (1987): 6- 8.

"Femme et Mathématique: quelles actions prendre?" in Bulletin d'association mathématique du Québec 27 (October 1987): 25-26.

"Women Scientists in Canada: The Need for Documentation," Resources for Feminist Research 15, no. 3. (November 1986): 7-8.

"D'assistantes anonymes a chercheures scientifiques: une rétrospective sur la place des femmes en sciences." Cahiers de recherche sociologique 4 (April 1986): 55-71.

"Lewis McIver Terrill -Promoter of Bird Study and Conservation in Quebec." Tchébec 12 (1982): 72-85.

"Henry Mousley and the Ornithology of Hatley and Montreal, 1910 1946." Tchébec 11 (1981): 113-134.

"The Contribution of the Amateur to North American Ornithology: A Historical Perspective." Living Bird 18 (1979 80): 161-77.

"Prey Piracy by Hawk-Owl on Common Crow." Tchébec 8 (1978): 93-97.

Publications (Other)

"Mabel Timlin, 1891-1976," p. 936 in Encyclopedia of Saskatchewan. Regina, Plains Research Centre, 2005.

Re-centering women in the landscape: A post-colonial feminist historian looks at gender, science and the environment in Canada." In Centering Women in the Landscape ed. by Daniela Stehlik, (Rockhampton: Central Queensland University, 2001), 13-36.

"Feminist Perspectives on Science and Technology," in "Building Inclusive Science" Ed. by Sue Rosser. Women's Studies Quarterly 28, No 1+ 2 (Spring/Summer 2000): 207-11.

"Science, Technology and Women's Lives," pp.9-18 in Andrea Rusnock, Syllabus Sampler: Women, Gender and the History of Science. Seattle, Washington: History of Science Society, 1999.

"Feminist Perspectives on Science and Technology," pp. 19-24 in Andrea Rusnock, Syllabus Sampler: Women, gender and the History of Science. Seattle, Washington: History of Science Society, 1999.

"Women's Studies is Wave of Future" Prince George Citizen, February 14, 1996.

"Mabel F. Timlin, FRSC (1891-1976)," in A Tribute to Mabel Timlin a special issue of the Canadian Women Economists Network Newsletter (November 1995): 1-4. "Mabel F. Timlin, FRSC (1891-1976). http://www. usask.ca/economics/timlin/sites.html.

"Canadian Achievements in Science - 35 biographies." Concordia University Science Exhibition, 1990.

"Women Scientists as Mothers-Conflict and/or Co-operation." pp. 73. In Mothering-Motherhood / Maternité-Maternage. ed. Pierre L'Hérault, 73-88. Montréal: Les Publication de l'Institut Simone de Beauvoir Institute Publications, 1990.

"One Hundred Years of Women and Science in Ontario." Crucible 21 (1990): 14-15.

"Women in Science: No More Stereotypes." Bridges (June/July 1989): 15-18.

"A Family of Women Scientists," Bulletin of the Simone de Beauvoir Institute 7, no.1 (1986): 5-10.

Works in Press

Catharine Parr Traill, 1802-1899. Dictionary of Scientific Biography.

Julia Wilmott Henshaw, 1869-1937. Dictionary of Canadian Biography.

"Science lessons for everyone? The writings of Catharine Parr Traill, 1802-1899," in Lorne Hammond ed. "Proceedings of the Joint Annual

Conference of the American Society of Environmental History and the National Council on Public History 2004.

"Alice Wilson, 1881-1964." Oxford Companion to Canadian History. Oxford University Press.

"E.W.R. Steacie, 1900-1962." Oxford Companion to Canadian History. Oxford University Press.

"William Rowan, 1891-1957." New Oxford Dictionary of National Biography. Oxford University Press.

Edith Berkeley, 1875-1963." New Oxford Dictionary of National Biography. Oxford University Press.

Works in Progress

Re-explorations: new perspectives on gender, environments, and the transfer of knowledge in 19th Century Canada, Australia and New Zealand.

Book Reviews (selected)

David Elliston Allen, "Naturalists and Society: The Culture of Natural History in Britain, 1700-1900." Annals of Science 62, 1 (January 2005), 125-127.

Margaret Lowman. "Life in the Treetops: Adventures of a Woman in Field Biology." Canadian Field- Naturalist 116, 3 (July-September): 508.

Gwyneth Hoyle, "Flowers in the Snow: The Life of Isobel Wylie Hutchinson." Beaver (February-March 2002): 48-49.

Paul L. Farber. "Discovering Birds: The Emergence of Ornithology as a Scientific Discipline, 1760-1850." Quarterly Journal of Biology 73 (June 1998): 194-95.

Debra Lindsay, ed., "The Modern Beginnings of Subarctic Ornithology. Northern Correspondence with the Smithsonian Institution, 1856-68." Canadian Historical Review (June 1997): 314-15.

John L. Cranmer-Byng. "A Life With Birds: Percy A. Taverner, Canadian Ornithologists, 1875-1947." Picoides 10 (Spring 1997): 11-12.

Margaret Gillett and Ann Beer, eds. "Our Own Agendas: Autobiographical Essays by Women Associated with McGill University." McGill Journal of Education 31, 3 (1996): 350-51.

Anne Montagnes, "Jade/Laverna," The Prince George Citizen June 29, 1996, 40.

Farley Kelly, ed. "On the Edge of Discovery: Australian Women in Science," Isis 86, 2 (1995): 304-305.

C. Kenneth Waters and Albert Van Helden, "Julian Huxley: Biologist and Statesman of Science." The Canadian Field-Naturalist 108 (1994): 388-89.

Trevor H. Levere, "Science and the Canadian Arctic. A Century of Exploration, 1818-1918." The Canadian Field-Naturalist 108 (1994): 132-133.

Marcia Myers Bonta, "Women in the Field: America's Pioneering Women Naturalists," The Canadian Field Naturalist 106 (1992): 548-549.

M. F. & G. W. Rayner-Canham, "Harriet Brooks: Pioneer Nuclear Scientist," The Queen's Quarterly 99, 3 (Fall 1992): 703-705.

Paul Russell Cutright, "Lewis & Clark: Pioneering Naturalists." The Canadian Field-Naturalist 105 (1991): 147.

Harriet Kofalk, "No Woman Tenderfoot: Florence Merriam Bailey, Pioneer Naturalist." The Canadian Field-Naturalist 104 (1990): 514.

D. R. Wiener, "Models of Nature: Ecology, Conservation, and Cultural Revolution in Soviet Russia." The Canadian Field- Naturalist 103 (1990): 467.

W. A. Waiser, "The Field Naturalist: John Macoun, the Geological Survey, and Natural Science." The Canadian Field-Naturalist 104 (1990): 336-37.

Luc Chartrand; Raymond Duchesne; Yves Gingras. "Histoire des sciences au Québec," Isis 80 (June 1989): 301 302.

Sandra Harding and Jean O. Barr, "Sex and Scientific Inquiry." The Canadian Journal of Sociology 14 (1989): 551-52.

Eva Vamos, "Women in Science: Options and Access," Technology and Culture (October 1989): 1085-86.

J. E. Bowers, "A Sense of Place: The Life and Work of Forrest Shreve." American Scientist 77 (September October 1989): 504.

P. Migdal Glazer and M. Slater, "Unequal Colleagues: The Entrance of Women into the Professions, 1890 1940," Journal of Higher Education 60 (January/February 1989): 116 18.

Peter J. Bowler, "Evolution: The History of an Idea." The Canadian Field-Naturalist 100 (1986): 452 453.

C. S. Houston, ed., "Arctic Ordeal. The Journal of John Richard¬son, Surgeon Naturalist with Franklin, 1820 22." The Canadian Field-Naturalist 99 (1985): 561.

Ann Hibner Koblitz, "A Convergence of Lives. Sofia Kovalevskaia: Scientist, Writer, Revolutionary." CAWIS News 3 (1984): 4.

Paul L. Farber, "The Emergence of Ornithology as a Scientific Discipline." The Auk 100 (1983): 763 65.

Ruth Tomalin, "W. H. Hudson A Biography." The Auk 100 (1983): 789 91.

"The Autobiography of John Macoun, Canadian Explorer and Naturalist, 1831 1920." The Canadian Field-Naturalist 96 (1982): 247 48.

Margaret Morse Nice, "Research is a Passion With Me." Ed. by Doris Huestis Speirs. Nature Canada 11 (1982): 50.

Robert A. Stebbins, "Amateurs: on the Margin Between Work and Leisure." Isis 72 (1981): 107

Invited Presentations

2006 - Gender, environments and the transfer of knowledge in 19th and 20th century Canada, Australia, and New Zealand. Curtin University, Perth, Western Australia, November 20, 2006.

2003 - Re-explorations: gender, science and the transfer of knowledge in 19th and 20th century Australia and Canada. Central Queensland University, Rockhampton, Qlnd. Australia. April 16, 2003 [VIDEO-TAPED].

2003 - Re-explorations: gender, environments and the transfer of aboriginal knowledge in 19th and 20th century Canada and Australia. History Program, Australian National University, Canberra, ACT, March 21, 2003.

2001 - "'Gynopia' at Work: Gendered Careers in Canadian Science." Institute for Research on Gender and Department of Sociology, Auckland University, New Zealand, March 28, 2001.

2001 - "Gender, Race and Science: comparative studies in Canada and New Zealand," Department of Sociology, Auckland University, New Zealand. March 29, 2001.

2001 - "Approaches in Studying Women and Science." History Department. Otago University, New Zealand, March 21, 2001.

2001 - "Re-explorations: gender, science, and environment in 19th and 20th century Canada, Australia, and New Zealand." History Department. Canterbury University. New Zealand. March 16, 2001.

2000 - "Women in the Landscape of Canadian Science," A Symposium on Gender, Science, and Environment, Central Queensland University, Rockhampton, Australia, June 23, 2000.

2000 - "Gendered Careers: Canadian women in science, 1890-1970." Women and Science series, St. John's College, University of British Columbia, March 14, 2000.

1999 - "Gendered careers: Canadian women science educators, 1890-1970." Centre for Teaching and Research on Women, McGill University. Montreal, October 6, 1999.

1998 - "Limited Horizons: Women Science Educators at Canadian Universities." Canadian History of Education Annual Conference. Vancouver, October 17, 1998

1998 - "Reinventing Ourselves." B. C. Women's Studies Association. Vancouver, May 2, 1998.

1998 - "Women Scientists and The Canadian Federation of University Women." CFUW, Prince George chapter. March 25, 1998.

1998 - "Despite the Odds Revisited: Reflections of the History of Canadian Women and Science." Simone de Beauvoir Institute, Concordia University. March 3, 1998.

1997 - "Feminist biography." English Program, UNBC, December 2, 1997.

1997 - "Beyond Statistics: What Can We Learn About Canadian Women in Science and Engineering?" Women's Advisory Committee, Revenue Canada, Prince George (two talks), October 16, 1997.

1997 - "Teaching the History of Canadian Science, Technology and Medicine--subversively." 10 Kingston Conference of the Canadian Science and Technology Historical Association, October 3, 1997-- session organizer Dr. Alain Canuel, SSHRC.

1997 - "How To Go About Doing Graduate Research?" Education Program, Faculty of Health and Human Sciences, UNBC, January 23, 1997.

1997 - History of Science Society Annual Conference [San Diego] "Women and Field Work in Canada: persistence and strategies, 1815-1990" for a special session on "Women Scientists in the Field" organized by Dr. Peggy Kidwell, Smithsonian Institution.

1996 - "Feminist Perspectives on an Integrated History of Canadian Science." History and Philosophy of Science, School of Science and Technology Studies, The University of New South Wales, May 10, 1996.

1996 - "Canadian Women in Science and Engineering: What Can We Learn From Our History?" History and Philosophy of Science and Technology, School of Science and Technology Studies, The University of New South Wales, May 14, 1996.

1996 - "The Ideal University -- or Can UNBC become/remain different from other Canadian universities?" UNBC Friday Forum series on the "Ideal University" February 9, 1996

1995 - Discussant, Alison Wylie, "Angles of Vision: The Engendering of Archaeology Past and Present." The Women, Gender and Science Question International Conference. Minneapolis, MN.

1994 "Science from the `Backwoods'?: Catharine Parr Traill (1802-1899) and Women's Science Writing in 19th-century Canada." History of Science Society Annual Conference, New Orleans, LA.

1994 - "Canadian Women in Science and Engineering." Department of Mechanical Engineering, Queen's University, Kingston, ON.

1994 - "An `Active Botanist': Catharine Parr Traill (1802-1899) and Women's Science Writing in Canada." Catharine Traill Naturalists' Club, Montreal, QC.

1993 - "Towards an integrated history of Canadian science."Lonergan University College, Concordia University, Montreal, QC.

1993 - "Transformations: A History of Canadian Women and Science." Association of Professional Engineers of Ontario, Toronto, ON.

1993 - "Canadian Women's Contributions to Chemistry." Women and Chemistry Symposium, Annual Meeting of the Chemical Institute of Canada, Sherbrooke, QC.

1993 - "Women and the Institutionalization of Science: What Can We Learn From Our History?" Faculty of Science, University of Manitoba, Winnipeg, MN.

1993 - "`Women's Work' in Geology: An Historical Perspective on Gender Division in Canadian Science." Women and Geoscience Symposium, University of Alberta, Edmonton, Alberta.

1992 - "Canadian Women in Science: What Can We Learn From Our History ?"5th CCWEST Conference, Toronto, ON.

1992 - "Despite the Odds Reconsidered: Careers for Women in Science and Engineering in Canada." History Department, Queen's University, Kingston, ON.

1991 - "`Women's Work' in Canadian science, 1890-1990." History Department, Queen's University, Kingston, ON.

1991 - "Plan for the Advancement of Women in Scholarship." Panel Discussion on the Royal Society of Canada's 1989 Report on the Advancement of Women in Scholarship. Concordia University, Montreal, QC.

1990 - "Women and the Institutionalization of Scientific Work in North America." Inaugural lecture, "Women in Science and Technology for Women" lecture series. Carleton University, Ottawa, ON.

1991 - "Women and Innovation." TSE Program, Carleton University, Ottawa, ON.

1991 - "Despite the Odds - Women in science." Women's Studies Program, John Abbott College, St. Anne de Bellevue, QC.

1991 - "`Women's work' in Chemistry: the Canadian Experience." Chemical Institute of Canada, Chemical Education Division, Halifax, N.S.

1991 - "Women and the Institutionalization of Scientific Work." History Department, Queen's University, Kingston, ON.

1991 - "Canadian Women Scientists--A Celebration." University Women's Club of Montreal, Montreal, QC.

1988 - "Rowan vs. Tory: Conflicting Views of Scientific Research in Canada, 1920 35." Department of the History of Science, Harvard University, Cambridge, MN.

1987 - "The Development of Scientific Disciplines in Canada." Panel Discussion, 5th Kingston Conference of the Canadian Science and Technology Historical Association, Ottawa, ON.

1987 - "Femme et mathématique: quelles actions prendre?" MOIFEM, Montreal, QC.

1979 - "Natural History to `Big Science': Two Centuries of Amateur Contributions to North American Ornithology." Laboratory of Ornithology, Cornell University, Ithaca, N.Y.

Conferences, Seminars, Talks

2004 - "Circulating gendered knowledge: Catharine Parr Traill's colonial science lessons, 1836-95," 5th Joint British-North American History of Science Conference, Halifax, NS.

2004 - "Science lessons for everyone? The writings of Catharine Parr

Traill, 1802-1899." Roundtable: The Walking Woman." Joint Annual Conference of the American Society of Environmental History and the National Council on Public History. Victoria, B.C,

2003 - "Marginal" landscapes of science? Gender, Environments, and Colonial Encounters in Nineteenth-century Australia, Canada, and New Zealand." 12th International Conference of Historical Geographers, Auckland, New Zealand.

2002 - "Colonial Lessons: Catherine Parr Traill (1802-99) and popular science education in Upper Canada." Canadian History of Education Association Conference, Quebec City, QC.

2000 - "Tracking Life Course Changes. Canadian Women in Science." Writing the Past Claiming the Future. St. Louis University, St. Louis, MI.

2000 - "Gendered Careers? Canadian Women in Science, 1890-1970." History of Science Society, Vancouver, B.C.

1999 - "Gendered Careers: Canadian Women as Science Educators, 1880-1970." 11th Kingston Conference on the Canadian Science and Technology Historical Association," ON.

1999 - "Women Science Educators and Canadian Universities, 1890-1970." Canadian Women Studies Association Conference, '99 Congress, Sherbrooke, QC.

1999 - "Women and Science at Canadian Universities, 1880-1960." 7th International Interdisciplinary Congress on Women, Tromso, Norway.

1998 - "Counteracting Gynopia: Research on the History of Canadian Women in Science and Engineering," Joint Session of the Canadian Women Studies Association and the History and Philosophy of Science Association, 98 Congress, Ottawa, ON.

1997 - "Beyond Statistics: A History of Canadian Women in Science and Engineering." 10 Kingston Conference of the Canadian Science and Technology Historical Association. Kingston, ON.

1996 - "Feminist Perspectives on Women, Science and Engineering in Canada: What Can We Learn From Our History?" Women and Other

Faces of Science Conference, University of Saskatchewan, Saskatoon, SK.

1996 - "Feminist Perspectives on Women, Science and Engineering in Canada." 6th International Interdisciplinary Congress on Women, The University of Adelaide, Adelaide, South Australia.

1995 - "Traditional Environmental Knowledge, Gender, and the `Spread of Western Science,' -- A Reappraisal of Basalla's Model." 9th Kingston Conference of the Canadian Science Technology Historical Association, Kingston, ON..

1995 - "Women and the Matthew Effect: A Century of Cumulative Disadvantages for Canadian Women in Science." The Woman, Gender and Science Question International Conference, Minneapolis, MN..

1993 - "(En)gendering Canadian science: Feminist Scientific Biography and the History of Canadian Science." History of Science Society Annual Conference, Santa Fe, N.M.

1993 - "Women and the Popularization of Science: 19th-century Women Science Writers in Canada," 8th Kingston Conference of the Canadian Science and Technology Historical Association, Kingston, ON.

1992 - "Laboratory Work in the Field Sciences in Canada: Gender Implications?" 2nd Joint British--North-American Conference on the History of Science, Toronto, ON.

1991 - "A Select Few: Women and the National Research Council of Canada," 7th Kingston Conference of the Canadian Science and Technology Historical Association, Ottawa, ON.

1991 - "Scientists vs. Government Experts: The Wood Buffalo Controversy, 1920-1990," 7th Kingston Conference of the Canadian Science and Technology Historical Association, Ottawa, ON.

1991 - "Introduction" to a Symposium on the History of Canadian Ornithology, American Ornithologists' Union Conference, Montreal, QC.

1991 - "William Rowan and the Transformation of Canadian Ornithology," Symposium on the History of Canadian Ornithology, American Ornithologists' Union Conference, Montreal, QC.

1991 - "Women and the Matthew Effect: A Century of Cumulative Disadvantages for Canadian Women in Science," Canadian Sociology and Anthropology Association Conference, Kingston, QC.

1989 - "Canadian Women Biologists, 1890 1970." 6th Kingston Conference of the Canadian Science and Technology Historical Association, Kingston, ON..

1989 - "The Hidden Dimension: Canadian Women and Science." Canadian Women Studies Association Conference, Quebec City, QC.

1987 - "Rowan vs. Tory : Two Approaches to Scientific Research."5th Kingston Conference of the Canadian Science and Technology Historical Association, Ottawa, ON..

1987 - "Researching `Women's Work' in Science: Some Methodological Problems," Simone de Beauvoir Institute, Concordia University Montreal, QC.

1986 - "William Rowan and the Experimental Approach in Ornithology," 19th International Ornithological Congress, Ottawa, ON.

1985 - "Last in the Field ? Canadian Women Natural Scientists   A pilot project." 4th Kingston Conference of the Canadian Science and Technology Historical Association, Kingston, ON.

1983 - "Women in North American Ornithology During the Last Century: A preliminary survey." First International Conference on the Role of Women in the History of Science, Technology and Medicine in the 19th and 20th centuries, Veszprém, Hungary.

1980 - "American Ornithology at Present: A new model for the functioning of a scientific discipline," History of Science Society, Toronto, ON.

1979 - "Amateurs and Professionals in North American Ornithology." Joint Atlantic Seminar for the History of Biology and Medicine, University of Toronto, ON.

1979 - "The Status of the Amateur in North American Ornithology." Institut d'histoire et de sociopolitique des sciences, Université de Montréal, Montreal, QC

Media Interviews

CBC Radio International, February 6, 2002

PGTV (Prince George), October 9, 1998

Concordia University, Thursday Report, October 2, 1998

CBC Home Run (Montreal), March 2, 1998

CBC (Montreal), June 20, 1998.

LaPresse (Montreal), October 4, 1997

CBC Daybreak (Prince George), January 18, 1996

CBC Calgary, May 1993

CBC Gabereau Show, January 1991

CTV News (Montreal), November 1990

CBC Morningside, August 1990

CBC Daybreak (Montreal), May 1990

CBC International (short-wave), March 1990

Selected Artworks by Marika

Muriwai View

Mt. Tolmie Sunset

Uluru

Facing Mt. Baker

Robin's Hood Bay

Meeting Place

Bamboo Watercolour

Only In Australia

Bird's Eye View of Tromsø

References

Margaret Pye Arnaudin, *A Bird in the Bush: the Story of the Province of Quebec Society for the Protection of Birds 1917-2002*. Price-Patterson Limited/Ltee, 2002.

Joseph Pasternak, *Cooking with Love and Paprika*, Bernard Geis, New York (1966)

"Eloges, Marianne (Marika) Gosztonyi Ainley, 1937-2008." Mary E. Baldwin. *Isis*, 2009, 100: 852-859.

Eavan Boland, "It's a Woman's World." This poem was first published in her poetry collection *Night Feed* (1982). It can also be found in *An Origin Like Water: Collected Poems 1967–1987* (1996).

Adriene Rich, "Planetarium," in *The Fact of a Doorframe: Selected Poems 1950-2001* (W. W. Norton and Company Inc., 2002).

Dorothy Livesay, "Bartok and the Geranium," in *New Poems by Dorothy Livesay*, Toronto: Emblem Books, 1955. 1st Edition.

Jacqueline Baldwin, *Professor Emerita: The Stander*, May 27, 2005.

Mary Catherine Bateson, *Composing a Life*. First published in 1989 by Grove/Atlantic, Inc. NY, re-issue in 2001.

Michelle Hoffman, *Historical Studies in Education / Revue d'histoire de l'éducation Historical*, 25, 2, Fall / automne 2013. Pg. 156-158.

Ruby Heap, *The Canadian Historical Review*, volume 94, no. 4, Dec. 2013, pp. 593-596 | 10.1353/can.2013.0077

Marika, Christmas on the Beach, Western Australia near Perth, 2006.

Made in the USA
Charleston, SC
18 October 2014